Machiavelli : the founder of the political science

John Morley
Thomas B. Macaulay

Machiavelli :
the Founder of the Political Science

LM Publishers

Who was Machiavelli?[1]

The greatest of the Florentines has likened
worldly fame to the breath of the wind that blows
now one way and now another way, and changes
name as it changes quarter. From every quarter, and
all the points of the historical compass, the veering
gusts of public judgment have carried incessantly
along from country to country and from generation
to generation, with countless mutations of aspect
and of innuendo, the sinister renown of
Machiavelli. Before he had been dead fifty years,
his name had become a byword and a proverb.
From Thomas Cromwell and Elizabeth; from the
massacre of St. Bartholomew, through League and
Fronde, through Louis XIV., Revolution, and
Empire, down to the third Napoleon and the days of
December; from the Lutheran Reformation down to
the blood and iron of Prince Bismarck; from
Ferdinand the Catholic down to Don Carlos; from
the Sack of Rome down to Gioberti, Mazzini, and
Cavour; in all the great countries all over the West,
this singular shade is seen haunting men's minds,
exciting, frightening, provoking, perplexing them,
like some unholy necromancer, bewildering reason

---

[1] By John Morley

and conscience by riddles and paradox. So far from withering or fading, his repute and his writings seem to attract deeper consideration as time goes on, and they have never been objects of more copious attention all over Europe than in the half-century that is now closing.

In the long and fierce struggle, from the fifteenth century onwards, among rival faiths and between contending forces in civil government, Machiavelli was hated and attacked from every side. In the great rising up of new types of life in the Church, and of life in the State, his name stood for something that partisans of old and new alike professed to abhor. The Church first tolerated, if it did not patronise, his writings; but soon, under the double stress of the Reformation in Germany on one hand, and the pagan Renaissance in Italy on the other, it placed him in that Index of forbidden books which now first (1557), in dread of the new art of printing, crept into formal existence. He speedily came to be denounced as schismatical, heretical, perverse, the impious foe of faith and truth. He was burnt in effigy. His book was denounced as written with the very fingers of Satan himself. The vituperation of the sixteenth century has never been surpassed either among learned or unlearned men, and the dead Machiavelli came in for his full share of unmeasured words. As Voltaire has said of Dante that his fame is secure because nobody reads him, so in an inverse sense, the bad name of Machiavelli grew worse, because men reproached, confuted, and cursed, but never read. Catholics attacked him as the enemy of the Holy See, and Protestants attacked him because he looked to a restoration of the spirit of ancient Rome, instead of a restoration of the faith and discipline of the primitive Church. While both of them railed at him, Catholic and Protestant each reviled the other as Machiavellist. In France national prejudice against the famous Italian queen-mother hit Machiavelli too, for his book was declared to be the oracle of Catherine de Medici, to whose father it was dedicated; it was held responsible for the Bartholomew massacre and the Huguenot wars. In Spain opposite ground was taken, and he who elsewhere was blamed as the advocate of persecution, was abominated here as the enemy of wars of religion, and the advocate of that monstrous thing, civil toleration. In England, royalists called him an atheist, and roundheads called him a Jesuit. A recent German writer has noted three hundred and ninety-five references to him in our Elizabethan literature, all fixing him with the craft, malice, and hypocrisy of the Evil One. Everybody knows how Hudibras finds in his Christian name the origin of our domestic title for the devil, though scholars have now long taught us to refer it to Nyke, the water-goblin of Norse mythology.

Some divines scented mischief in the comparative method, and held up their hands at the impudent wickedness that dared to find a parallel between people in the Bible and people in profane history, between King David and Philip of Macedon. Whenever a bad name floated into currency, it was flung at Machiavelli, and his own name was counted among the worst that could be flung at a bad man. Averroes for a couple of centuries became a conventional label for a scoffer and an atheist, and Machiavelli, though he cared no more for the abstract problems that exercised the Moslem thinker, than he would have cared for the inward sanctities of Thomas à Kempis, was held up to odium as an Averroist. The Annals of Tacitus were discovered: his stern ironies on Tiberius and the rest did not prevent one school of politicians from treating his book as a manual for tyrants, while another school applied it against the Holy Roman Empire; his name was caught up in the storms of the hour, and Machiavellism and Tacitism became convertible terms.

It is not possible here to follow the varying fates of Machiavelli's name and books. The tale of Machiavellian criticism in our own century is a long one. That criticism has followed the great stream of political events in continental Europe; for it is events after all that make the fortune of books, rather than books that create events. Revolutions in France, unification in Italy, unification in Germany, the disappearance of the Temporal Power, the activity of the principle of Nationality, the realisation of the idea of the Armed People, have all in turn and in different forms raised the questions to which Machiavelli gave such daring point. On the medallion that commemorates him in the church of Santa Croce, are the words, *Tanto nomini nullum par elogium*, So great a name no praise can match. We only need to think of Michelangelo and Galileo reposing near him, in order to realise the extravagance of such a phrase, and to understand that reaction in his favour has gone as intolerably far as the old diatribes against him.

It may be doubted whether in this country Machiavelli has ever been widely read. Thomas Cromwell, the powerful minister of Henry VIII., the *malleus monachorum*, told Cardinal Pole that he had better fling aside dreamers like Plato, and read a new book by an ingenious Italian which treated the arts of government practically. Cromwell in his early wanderings had been more than once in Italy, and he was probably at Florence at the very time when Machiavelli was writing his books at his country farm But a more shining figure in English history than Cromwell, was even more profoundly attracted by the genius of Machiavelli, and this was Bacon. It was natural that his vast and comprehensive genius should admire the extension to the sphere of civil government, of the same method which he was advocating in the investigation of external nature. 'We are much beholden,' he said, 'to Machiavel and others that wrote what men do, and not what they ought to do.' The rejection of *a priori* and abstract principles, and of authority as the test of truth, the substitution of chains of observed fact for syllogism with major premiss unproved—this revolution in method could not be reserved, for one department of thought. Bacon's references are mainly to the *Discourses* and not to the *Prince*, but he had well digested both. The *Essays* bear the impress of Machiavelli's positive spirit, and Bacon's ideal of history is his. 'Its true office is to represent the events themselves, together with the counsels, and to leave the observations and conclusions thereupon to the liberty and faculty of every man's judgment.' His own history of Henry VII. is a good example of such a life as Machiavelli would have written of such a hero.

The most powerful English thinker of Machiavelli's political school is Hobbes. He drew similar lessons from a similar experience—the distractions of Civil War at home, and the growth, which he watched during many years of exile, of centralised monarchy abroad. Less important is Harrington, whose *Oceana* or model of a commonwealth was once so famous, and is in truth one of the most sensible productions of that kind of literature. Harrington travelled in Italy, was much at home with Italian politics and books on politics, and perhaps studied Machiavelli more faithfully than any other of his countrymen. He tells us, writing after the Restoration, that his works had then fallen into neglect. Scattered through the *Patriot King* and other writings of Bolingbroke are half a dozen references to Machiavelli, but they have the air, to use a phrase of Bacon's, of being but cloves stuck in to spice the dish, and the Italian's pregnant thinking has no serious place in an author whose performances are little more than splendid beating of the wind. Hume had evidently read the *Discourses*, the *Prince*, and the *History of Florence* with attention, and with his usual faculty for hitting the nail on the head, he avows a suspicion that the world is still too young to fix many general truths in politics. We have not as yet had experience of 3000 years. We do not know of what great changes human nature may show itself susceptible, nor what great revolutions may come about in men's customs and principles.

It would take a long chapter to draw a full comparison between Machiavelli and Montesquieu, who was undoubtedly set by him on some trains of thinking both in his short book on the Romans, and his more memorable book on Laws. It may be too much to say, as some critics have said, that all the great modern ideas have their beginning in Montesquieu. But this is at least true among other marked claims that might be made for him, that in spite of much looseness of definition and a thousand imperfections in detail, he launched effectually on European thought the conception of social phenomena as being no less subject to general laws than all other phenomena. Of a fundamental extension of this kind, Machiavelli was in every way incapable, nor did the state of any of the sciences at that date permit it. As for secondary differences it is enough to say that Machiavelli put the level of human character low, and Montesquieu put it high; that one was always looking to fact, the other to idea; that one was sombre, the other buoyant, cheerful, and an optimist; Montesquieu confident in the moral forces of mankind, Machiavelli leaving moral forces out, and not knowing where to look for them. Finally, 'Montesquieu's book is a study, Machiavelli's is a political act, an attempt at political resurrection.'

When Machiavelli turned to serious writing, he was five-and-forty (b.1469). His life had been interesting and important. For fifteen years he held the post of secretary of one of the departments in the government of Florence, where he was brought into close relations with some of the most remarkable personages and events of his time. He went four times on a mission to the King of France; he was with Cæsar Borgia in the ruthless campaign of 1502; he did the business of his republic with Pope Julius II at Rome, and with the Emperor Maximilian at Innsbruck. The modern practice of resident ambassadors had not yet established itself in the European system, and Machiavelli was never more than an envoy of secondary rank. But he was

14

in personal communication with sovereigns and ministers, and he was a watchful observer of all their ways and motives. We need not here concern ourselves with all the chances and changes of Italian policies in the fifteenth and sixteenth centuries. In the long struggle between freedom and tyranny in his native Florence, Machiavelli belonged to the popular party. When they fell in 1512, and when the Medici returned, he was turned out of his post, thrown into prison, put to the question with ropes and pulleys, according to the fashion of the time, shared the benefit of the amnesty accorded when Leo X. ascended the papal throne, and withdrew to San Casciano. This was the time when he composed most of the writings that have made him famous. Here is his picture of himself, in a letter to a friend (December 10, 1513):—

"I am at my farm; and, since my last misfortunes, have not been in Florence twenty days. I rise with the sun, and go into a wood of mine that is being cut, where I remain two hours inspecting the work of the previous day and conversing with the woodcutters, who have always some trouble on hand among themselves or with their neighbours. When I leave the wood, I proceed to a well, and thence to the place which I use for snaring birds, with a book under my arm—Dante, or Petrarch, or one of the minor poets, like Tibullus or Ovid. I read the story of their passions, and let their loves remind me of my own, which is a pleasant pastime for a while. Next I take the road, enter the inn door, talk with the passers-by, inquire the news of the neighbourhood, listen to a variety of matters, and make note of the different tastes and humours of men. This brings me to dinner-time, when I join my family and eat the poor produce of my farm. After dinner I go back to the inn, where I generally find the host and a butcher, a miller, and a pair of bakers. With these companions I play the fool all day at cards or backgammon: a thousand squabbles, a thousand insults and abusive dialogues take place, while we haggle over a farthing, and shout loud enough to be heard from San Casciano. But when evening falls I go home and enter my writing-room. On the threshold I put off my country habit, filthy with mud and mire, and array myself in royal courtly garments; thus worthily attired, I make my entrance into the ancient courts of the men of old, where they receive me with love, and where I feed upon that food which only is my own and for which I was born. I feel no shame in conversing with them and asking them the reason of their actions. They, moved by their humanity, make answer; for four hours' space I feel no annoyance, forget all care; poverty cannot frighten, nor death appal me. I am carried away to their society. And since Dante says "that there is no science unless we retain what we have learned," I have set down what I have gained from their discourse, and composed a treatise, De

Principatibus, in which I enter as deeply as I can into the science of the subject, with reasonings on the nature of principality, its several species, and how they are acquired, how maintained, how lost. If you ever liked any of my scribblings, this ought to suit your taste. To a prince, and especially to a new prince, it ought to prove acceptable. Therefore I am dedicating it to the Magnificence of Giuliano."

Machiavelli was not meant either by temperament or principle to be a willing martyr. Not for him was the stern virtue of Dante, who accepted lifelong exile rather than restoration with dishonour, content from any corner of the earth to wonder at the sun and the stars, and under any sky to meditate all sweetest truths (*le dolcissime verità*). Not for the ambitious and practical politician was the choice of Savonarola, who, at the moment when Machiavelli was crossing the threshold of public life, had perished at the stake, rather than cease from his warnings that no good could come to Florence save from the fear of God and the reform of manners. Nobody had in him less of the Stoic; his private character was not more austere than the Italian morality of his day; his purse was painfully lean; his active and restless mind suffered from that 'malady of lost power' which, they say, is apt to afflict members of Opposition, and he longed to be back in the business of the State. So he dedicated his book to Lorenzo, in the hope that such speaking proof of his experience and capacity would induce the destroyers of the freedom of his city to give him public employment. His suppleness did not pay. Nothing came of the dedication for several years. Then some trivial duties were found for Machiavelli, and one important literary task was intrusted to him, the history of Florence. This he completed and dedicated to Leo X. in 1527. To the same period belongs a comedy which some have described as worthy of Aristophanes, and hardly second to the *Tartufe* of Molière. Like Bacon and some others who have written the shrewdest things on human conduct and the arts of success, he had made a sorry mess of his own chances and gifts. It is always interesting to watch how men take the ill-usage of the world and the miscarriages of life. Machiavelli's was one of those grave intellects, apt for serious thought, yet which easily turn to levity, console themselves for failure by mockery of themselves, and repay Fortune with her own banter. This is the vein of the brilliant burlesque and satire with which this versatile genius diversified his closing days. Still, with indomitable perseverance he clung to public things, and he now composed the dialogues on the Art of War, to induce his countrymen to substitute for mercenary armies a national militia—to-day one of the organic ideas of the European system. *Amo la patria mia più dell' anima*, he wrote to a friend just before his death, and one view of Machiavelli is that he was always the lion masquerading in the fox's skin, an impassioned patriot, under all his craft and jest and bitter mockery. Even Mazzini, who explained the ruin of Italy by the fact that Machiavelli prevailed over Dante, admits that he had 'a profoundly Italian heart.' In 1527 he died.

Machiavelli's active life, then, was passed in council-chambers, camps, courts; he pondered over what he had seen in the light of the few books that be had read,—Livy, Polybius, Tacitus, some portion of Aristotle's *Politics*, Dante, Petrarch. Nobody borrowed more, and yet few are more original. If he had ever read Thucydides, he would have recalled that first great chapter in European literature, still indeed the greatest in its kind, of reflections on a revolution, where with incomparable insight and fidelity the historian analyses the demoralisation of the Hellenic world, as it lay a prey to intestine faction and the ruinous invocation of foreign aid. These terrible calamities, says Thucydides, always have been and always will be, while human nature remains the same. Words cease to have the same relations to things, and their meanings are changed, to suit the ingenuities of enterprise and the atrocities of revenge. Frantic energy is the quality most valued, and the man of violence is always trusted. That simplicity which is a chief ingredient of a noble nature, is laughed to scorn. Inferior intellects succeed best. Revenge becomes dearer than self-preservation, and men even have a sweeter pleasure in the revenge that goes with perfidy, than if it were open. All this was just as true of Florence in the sixteenth century, as it was of Athens, Corinth, and Corcyra in the fifth century before Christ. The postulate of Thucydides, that human nature should remain the same, still held good, as it has held good at many a stormful period since, the social progress of the ages notwithstanding.

Whether the moral state of Italy was intrinsically and substantially worse than that of other European nations, is a question which those who know most, are least disposed to answer offhand. Still Italy presents some peculiarities that shed over her civilisation at this time a curious and deadly iridescence. Passions moved in strange orbits. Private depravity and political debasement went with one of the most brilliant intellectual awakenings in the history of the western world. Another dark element is the association of merciless selfishness, violence, craft, and corruption with the administration of sacred things. If politics were divorced from morals, so was theology. Modem conscience is shocked by the resort to hired crime and stealthy assassination, especially by poison. Mariana, the famous Spanish Jesuit, tells us (*De Rege*, i. 7) that when he was teaching theology in Sicily (1567), a certain young prince asked him whether it were lawful to slay a tyrant by poison. The theologian did not find it easy to draw a distinction between poison and steel, but at last he fell upon a reason (and a most absurd reason it is) for his decision that a poniard is permitted and white powder is not. What distinguishes the Italian Renaissance from such epochs of luxury and corruption as the French Regency, is this contempt of human life, the fury of private revenge, the spirit of atrocious perfidy and crime. 'Italian society admired the bravo almost as much as Imperial Rome admired the gladiator: it assumed that genius combined with force of character released men from the shackles of ordinary morality' (Symonds). Only a giant like Michelangelo escaped this deadly climate. We see the violence of Michelangelo's sublime despair in the immortal marbles of the Medicean chapel, executed while Machiavelli was still alive— Lorenzo, to whom the *Prince* is dedicated, silent, pensive, meditating under his helmet, with finger upon lip, some stroke of dubious war or craft, and the sombre superhuman figures of Night and Dawn and Day, proclaiming 'it is best to sleep and be of stone, not to see and not to feel, while such misery and shame endure.'

Machiavelli's merit in the history of political literature is his method. We may smile at the uncritical simplicity with which he discusses Romulus and Remus, Moses, Cyrus, and Theseus, as if they were all astute politicians of Florentine faction. He often recalls the orator in the French Constituent Assembly who proposed to send to Crete for an authentic copy of the laws of Minos. But he withdrew politics from scholasticism, and based their consideration upon observation and experience. It is quite true that he does not classify his problems; that he does not place them in their proper subordination to one another; that he often brings together facts that are not of the same order and do not support the same conclusion. Nothing, again, is easier than for the critic to find contradictions in Machiavelli. He was a man of the world reflecting over the things that he had seen in public life; more systematic than observers like Retz or Commynes—whom Sainte-Beuve calls the French Machiavelli—but not systematic as Hobbes is. Human things have many sides and many aspects, and an observant man of the world does not confine himself to one way of looking at them, from fear of being thought inconsistent. To put on the blinkers of system was alien to his nature and his object. Contradictions were inevitable, but the general texture of his thought is close enough.

Machiavelli was not the first of his countrymen to write down thoughts on the problems of the time, though it has been observed that he is the first writer, still celebrated, 'who discussed grave questions in modern language' (*Mackintosh*). Apart from Dante and Petrarch, various less famous men had theorised about affairs of state. Guicciardini, the contemporary and friend of Machiavelli, like him a man of public business and of the world, composed observations on government, of which Cavour said that they showed a better comprehension of affairs than the author of the *Prince* and the *Discourses*. But then the latter had the better talent of writing. One most competent Italian critic calls his prose 'divine,' and a foreigner has perhaps no right to differ; only what word is then left for the really great writers, who to intellectual strength add moral grandeur? Napoleon hated a general who made mental pictures of what he saw, instead of looking at the thing clearly as through a field-glass. Machiavelli's is the style of the field-glass. 'I want to write something,' he said, 'that may be useful to the understanding man; it seems better for me to go behind to the real truth of things, rather than to a fancy picture.' Every sentence represents a thought or a thing. He is never open to the reproach thrown by Aristotle at Plato: 'This is to talk poetic metaphor.' As has been said much less truly of Montesquieu, reflection is not broken by monuments and landscapes. He has the highest of all the virtues that prose-writing can possess—save the half-dozen cases in literature of genius with unconquerable wings,—he is simple, unaffected, direct, vivid, and rational. He possesses the truest of all forms of irony, which consists in literal statement, and of which you are not sure whether it is irony or *naïveté*. He disentangles his thought from the fact so skilfully and cleanly, that it looks almost obvious. Nobody has ever surpassed him in the power of throwing pregnant vigour into a single concentrated word. Of some pages it has been well said that they are written with the point of a stiletto. He uses few of our loud easy words of praise and blame, he is not often sorry or glad, he does not smile and he does not scold, he is seldom indignant and he is never surprised. He has not even the mastering human infirmity of trying to persuade. His business is that of the clinical lecturer, explaining the nature of the malady, the proper treatment, and the chances of recovery. He strips away the flowing garments of convention and commonplace; closes his will against sympathy and feeling; ignores pity as an irrelevance, just as the operating surgeon does. In the phrase about Fontenelle, he shows as good a heart as can be made out of brains. What concerns Machiavelli, the Italian critic truly says, 'is not a thing being reasonable, or moral, or beautiful, but that it is.' Yet at the bottom of all the confused clamour against him, people knew what they meant, and their instinct was not unsound. Mankind, and well they know it, are far too profoundly concerned in right and wrong, in mercy and cruelty, in justice and oppression, to favour a teacher who, even for a scientific purpose of his own, forgets the awful difference. Commonplace, after all, is exactly what contains the truths that are indispensable.

Like most of those who take a pride in seeing human nature as it is, Machiavelli only saw half of it. We must remember the atmosphere of craft, suspicion, fraud, violence, in which he had moved, with Borgias, Medici, Pope Julius, Maximilian, Louis XII., and the reckless factions of Florence. His estimate was low. Mankind are more prone to evil than to good. We may say this of them generally, that they are ungrateful, fickle, deceivers, greedy of gain, runaways before peril. While you serve them, they are all yours—lives, goods, children—so long as no danger is at hand; but when the hour of need draws nigh, they turn their backs. They are readier to seek revenge for wrong, than to prove gratitude for service: as Tacitus says of people who lived in Italy long ages before, readier to pay back injury than kindness. Men never do anything good, unless they are driven; and where they have their choice, and can use what licence they will, all is filled with disorder and confusion. They are taken in by appearances. They follow the event. They easily become corrupted. Their will is weak. They know not how to be either thoroughly good or thoroughly bad; they vacillate between; they take middle paths, the worst of all. Men are a little breed.

All this is not satire, it is not misanthropy; it is the student of the art of government, thinking over the material with which he has to deal. These judgments of Machiavelli have none of the wrath of

Juvenal, none of the savage truculence of Swift. They cut deeper into simple reality than the polished proverbs of the moralists of the boudoir. They have not the bitterness that hides in the laugh of Molière, nor the chagrin and disdain with which Pascal broods over unhappy man and his dark lot. Least of all are they the voice of the preacher calling sinners to repentance. The tale is only a rather grim record, from inspection, of the foundations on which the rulers of states must do their best to build.

Goethe's maxim that, if you would improve a man, it is no bad thing to let him suppose that you already think him that which you would have him to be, would have seemed to Machiavelli as foolish for his purpose as if you were to furnish an architect with clay, and bid him to treat it as if it were iron. He will suffer no abstraction to interrupt positive observation. Man is what he is, and so he needs to be bitted and bridled with laws, and now and again to be treated to a stiff dose of ' *medicine forti* ' in the shape of fire, bullet, axe, halter, or dungeon. At any rate, Machiavelli does not leave human nature out, and this is one secret of his hold. He does not argue pale opinions, but passions and interests in all the flush of their action. It is, in truth, in every case,— Burke, Rousseau, Tocqueville, Hobbes, Bentham, Mill, and the rest—always the moralist who interests men most within the publicist. Machiavelli was assuredly a moralist, though of a peculiar sort,

26

and this is what makes him, as he has been called, a contemporary of every age and a citizen of all countries.

To the question whether the world grows better or worse, Machiavelli gave an answer that startles an age like ours, that lives on its faith in progress. The world neither grows better nor worse; in fact it is always the same. Human fortunes are never still; they are every moment either going up or sinking down. But among all nations and states, the same desires, the same humours prevail, and are what they always were. Men are for travelling on the beaten track. Diligently study bygone things, and in every State you will be able to discover the things to come. All the things that have been may be again. Just as the modern physicist tells us that neither physical nor chemical transformation changes the mass nor the weight of any quantity of matter, so Machiavelli judged the good and evil in the world to be ever the same. 'This bad and this good shift from land to land,' he says, 'as we may see from ancient empires; they rose and fell with the changes of their usage, but the world remained as it was. The only difference was that it concentrated its power (*virtù*) in Assyria, then in Media, then in Persia, until at last it came to Italy and Rome.'

In our age, when we think of the chequered course of human time, of the shocks of irreconcilable civilisations, of war, trade, faction, revolution, empire, laws, creeds, sects, we seek a clue to the vast maze of historic and pre-historic fact. Machiavelli seeks no clue to his distribution of good and evil. He never tries to find a moral interpretation for the mysterious scroll. We obey laws that we do not know, but cannot resist. We can only make an effort to seize events as they whirl by, and to extort from them a maxim, a precept, or a principle, to serve our immediate turn. Fortune, he says,—that is, Providence, or else Circumstance, or the Stars,—is mistress of more than half we do. What is her deep secret, he shows no curiosity to fathom. He contents himself with a maxim for the practical man (*Prince*, xxv.), that it is better to be adventurous than cautious, for Fortune is a woman, and to be mastered must be boldly handled.

Whatever the force or the law that may control this shifting distribution of imperial destinies, nothing, said Machiavelli, could prevent any native of Italy or of Greece, unless the Greek had turned Turk, or the Italian had turned Transalpine, from blaming his own time, and praising the glories of time past. 'What,' he cries, 'can redeem an age from the extremity of misery, shame, reproach, where there is no regard to religion, to laws, to arms, where all is tainted and tarnished with every foulness. And these vices are all the more hateful, as they most abound in those who sit in the judgment-seat, are men's masters, and seek men's reverence. I, at all events,' he concludes, with a

28

glow so rare in him, that almost recalls the moving close of the *Agricola*, 'shall make bold to say how I regard old times and new, so that the minds of the young, who shall read these writings of mine, may shun the new examples and follow the old. For it is the duty of a good man, at least to strive to teach to others those sound lessons, which the spite of time or fortune hath hindered him from executing, to the end that many having learned them, some one of those better loved by heaven may one day have power to apply them.'

What were the lessons? They were in fact only one, that the central secret of the ruin and distraction of Italy was weakness of will, want of fortitude, force, and resolution. The abstract question of the best form of government—perhaps the most barren of all the topics that have ever occupied speculative minds—was with Machiavelli strictly secondary. He saw small despotic states harried by their petty tyrants, he saw republics worn out by faction and hate. Machiavelli himself had faith in free republics as the highest type of government; but whether you have republic or tyranny, matters less, he seems to say, than that the governing power should be strong in the force of its own arms, intelligent, concentrated, resolute. He might be said to be for half his time engaged in examining the fitness of means to other people's ends, himself neutral. But then, as nature used to be held to abhor a vacuum, so the impatience of man is loth to tolerate neutrality. He has been charged with inconsistency because in the *Prince* he lays down the conditions on which an absolute ruler, rising to power by force of genius backed by circumstances, may maintain that power, with safety to himself and most advantage to his subjects; while in the *Discourses* he examines the rules that enable a self-governing state to retain its freedom. The cardinal precepts are the same. In either case, the saving principle is one: self-sufficiency, military strength, force, flexibility, address,—above all, no half-measures. In either case, the preservation of the state is equally the one end, reason of state equally the one adequate and sufficient test and justification of the means. The *Prince* deals with one problem, the *Discourses* with the other, but the spring of Machiavelli's political inspirations is the same, to whatever type of rule they apply—the secular state supreme; self-interest, and self-regard, avowed as the single principles of state action; material force the master-key to civil policy. Clear intelligence backed by unsparing will, unflinching energy, remorseless vigour, the brain to plan and the hand to strike—here is the salvation of States, whether monarchies or republics. The spirit of humility and resignation that Christianity had brought into the world, he contemns and repudiates. That whole scheme of the Middle Ages in which invisible Powers rule all our mortal affairs, he dismisses. Calculation, courage, fit means for resolute ends, human force,—only these can rebuild a world in ruins.

Some will deem it inconsistent, that with so few illusions about the weaknesses of human nature, yet he should have been so firm, in what figures in all our own election addresses as trust in the people. Like Aristotle, he held the many to be in the long-run the best judges; but unlike Goethe, who said that the public is always in a state of self-delusion about details, though scarcely ever about broad truths, Machiavelli declared that the public may go wrong about generalities, while as to particulars they are usually right. The people are less ungrateful than a prince, and where they are ungrateful, it is from less dishonourable motive. The multitude is wiser and more constant than a prince. Furious and uncontrolled multitudes go wrong, but then so do furious and uncontrolled princes. Both err, when not held back by fear of consequences. The people are fickle and thankless, but so are princes. 'As for prudence and stability, I say that a people is more prudent, more stable, and of better judgment than a prince.' Never let a prince, he said—and perhaps we might say, never let a parliament of united kingdoms—complain of the faults of a people under his rule, for they are due either to his own negligence, or else to his own example, and if you consider a people given to robbery and outrages against law, you will generally find that they only copy their masters.

Above all, and in any case, the ruler, whether hereditary or an usurper, can have no safety unless he founds himself on popular favour and good-will. This he repeats a hundred times. 'Better far than any number of fortresses, is not to be hated by your people.'

It is then to the free Roman commonwealth that Machiavelli would have his countrymen turn. He found the pattern that he wanted in that strong respect for law, that devotion to country, that unquailing courage, that energy of purpose, which has been truly called the essence of free Rome. Modern Germans, for good reasons of their own, have taken to praise him, but Machiavelli has nothing to do with that most brilliant and illustrious of living German scholars, who idolises Julius Cæsar, despatches Cato as a pedant, and Cicero as a coxcomb. You will hardly find in Machiavelli a good word for any destroyer of a free government. Let nobody, he says, be cheated by the glory of Cæsar. Historians have been spoiled by his success, and by the duration of the empire that continued his name. If you follow the history of the empire, you will then know with a vengeance what is the debt of Rome, Italy, and the world, to Cæsar.

Nobody has stated the argument against the revolutionary dictator more clearly or tersely than Machiavelli. He applauded the old Romans because their policy provided by a regular ordinance for an emergency, by the institution of a constitutional dictator for a fixed term, and to meet a definite occasion. 'In a republic nothing should be left to extraordinary modes of government; because though such a mode may do good for the moment, still the example does harm, seeing that a practice of breaking the laws for good ends lends a colour to breaches of law for ends that are bad.' Occasions no doubt arise when no ordinary means will produce reform, and then you must have recourse to violence and arms: a man must make himself supreme. But then, unfortunately, if he make himself supreme by violence, he is probably a bad man, for a good man will not climb to power by such means. No more will a bad man who has become supreme in this way be likely to use his ill-gotten power for good ends. Here is the eternal dilemma of a State in convulsion.

He forbids us in any case to call it virtue to slay fellow-citizens, to betray friends, to be without faith, without mercy, without religion; such practices may win empire, but not glory. A prince who clears out a population—here we may think of James I. and Cromwell, and the authors of many a sweeping clearance since—and transplants them from province to province, as a herdsman moves his flock, does what is most cruel, most alien, not only to Christianity, but to common humanity. It were far better for a man, he says, to choose a private life, than to be a king on the terms of making such havoc as this with the lives of other men (*Disc.*, i. 26).

It may be true, as Danton said, that 'twere better to be a poor fisherman than to meddle with the government of men. Yet nations and men find themselves inexorably confronted by the practical question. Government they must find. Given a corrupt, a divided, a distracted community, how are you to restore it? The last chapter of the *Prince* is an eloquent appeal to the representative of the House of Medici to heal the bruises and bind up the wounds of his torn and enslaved country. The view has been taken that this last chapter has nothing to do with the fundamental ideas of the book; that its glow is incompatible with the iron harshness of all that has gone before; that it was an afterthought, dictated partly by Machiavelli's personal hopes, and then picked up later by his defenders as whitewashing guilty maxims by ascribing them to large and lofty purpose. The balance of argument seems to me to lean this way, and Machiavelli for five-and-twenty chapters was thinking of new princes generally, and not of a great Italian deliverer. At the same time, he was not a man cast in a single mould. It may be that on reviewing his chapters, his heart became suddenly alive to their frigidity, and that the closing words flowed from the deeps of what was undoubtedly sincere and passionate feeling.

However this may be, whether the whole case of Italy or the special case of any new prince, was in his contemplation, the quality of the man required is drawn in four chapters (xv.-xviii.) with piercing eye and a hand that does not flinch. The ruler's business is to save the State. He cannot practise all virtues, first because he is not very likely to possess them, and next because, where so many people are bad, he would not be a match for the world if he were perfectly good. But he should be on his guard against all vices, so far as possible; he should at all events scrupulously abstain from every vice that might endanger his government. There are two ways of carrying on the fight—one by laws, the other by force. The first is the proper distinction of man; the second is the mark of the brute. As the first is not always enough, you must sometimes resort to the second. You must be both lion and fox, and the man who is only lion, is not wise. A wise prince neither can, nor ought to, keep his word, when to keep his word would injure either himself or the State, or when the reasons that made him give his promise have passed away. If men were all good, such a maxim as this would be bad; but as men are inclined to evil, and would not all keep faith with you, why should you keep faith with them? *Nostra cattività, la lor*—our badness, their badness. There are some good qualities which the new ruler need not have, still he should appear to have them. It is well to appear merciful, faithful, religious, and to be so. Religion is the most necessary thing of all for a prince to seek credit for. But the new prince should know how to change to the contrary of all these things, when they are in the way of the public good. For it is frequently necessary—and here is the sentence that has done so much to damn its writer—for the upholding of the State, to go to work against faith, against charity, against humanity, against religion; and a new prince cannot observe all the things for which men are reckoned good.

The property of his subjects he will leave alone, for a man will sooner forgive the slaying of his father than the confiscation of his patrimony. He should try to have a character for mercy, but this should never be allowed to prevent severity on just occasion. He must bear in mind the good saying reported in Livy, that many people know better how to keep from doing wrong, than how to correct the wrongdoing of others. He ought not to let excess of trust make him careless, nor excess of distrust to make him intolerable. It would be well if he could be both loved and feared; but, if circumstances force a choice, then it is better that he should be feared. To be feared is not the same as being hated, and the two things to be most avoided are hatred on the one hand, and contempt on the other.

The universal test is reason of State. We should never condemn a man for extraordinary acts to which he has been compelled to resort in establishing his empire or founding a republic. In a case where the safety of a country is concerned, whether it be princedom or republic, no regard ought to be paid to justice or injustice, to pity or severity, to glory or shame; but putting aside every other consideration, that course alone ought to be followed which may preserve to the country its existence and its freedom. Diderot pithily put the superficial impression of all this when he said that you might head these chapters as 'The circumstances under which it is right for a Prince to be a Scoundrel.' A profounder commentary of a concrete kind is furnished by Mommsen's account of Sulla—an extraordinary literary masterpiece, even in the view of those who think its politics most perverse. Such a Sulla was the real type of Machiavelli's reformer of a rotten State.

It has been a commonplace of reproachful criticism that Machiavelli chose for his hero Cæsar Borgia. Not only was Borgia a monster, it is said, but he failed. The baleful meteor flamed across the sky for little more than four years, and then went out. If only success should command admiration, Borgia and his swiftly shattered fortunes ought to be indifferent to Machiavelli and the world for which he was writing. What Machiavelli says is this—'I put him forward,' he writes, 'as a model for

37

such as climb to power by good fortune and the help of others. He did everything that a long-headed and capable man could do, who desires to strike root. I will show you how broad were the foundations that he laid for the fabric of his future power. I do not know what better lessons I could teach a new prince (*i.e.* an usurper) than his example. If what he did failed in the end, it was all due to the extreme malignity of fortune.' He makes no hero of him, except as a type of character well fitted for a given task.

Machiavelli knew him at close quarters. He was sent on a mission to Borgia in the crisis of his fortunes, and he saw in him the very qualities of action, force, combat, calculation, resolution, that the weakness of the age required. Machiavelli was in his train when terrible things were done. Cæsar was close, solitary, secret, quick. When any business is on foot, said Machiavelli, he knows nothing of rest or weariness or risk. He no sooner reached a place, than you heard that he had left it. He was loved by his troopers, for though he meted stern punishment for every offence against discipline, he was liberal in pay, and put little restraint on their freedom. Though no talker, when he had to make a case he was so fluent and pressing, that it was hard to find an answer. He was a great judge of occasion. Bold, crafty, resolute, deep, and above all well known never to forget or forgive an injury, he fascinated men with the terror of the basilisk. His firm maxim was to seek order by giving his new subjects a good and firm government, including a civil tribunal with a just president. Remiro was his first governor in the Romagna. It is uncertain how Remiro incurred his master's displeasure, but one morning Machiavelli walked out into the market-place at Cesena, and saw Remiro, as he puts it, in two pieces, his head on a lance, and his body still covered with his fine clothes, resting on a block with a blood-stained axe by the side of it. His captains, beginning to penetrate Cæsar's designs, and fearing that he would seize their petty dominions—like the leaves of an artichoke, as he said—one by one, revolted. Undaunted, he gathered new forces. Fresh bands of mercenaries flocked to the banners of a chief who had money, skill, and a happy star. The conspirators were no match for him in swiftness, activity, or resources; they allowed him to sow the seeds of disunion among them; he duped them into making a convention with him, which they had little thought of keeping. Everybody who knew his revengeful and implacable spirit was sure that the conspirators were doomed. When Machiavelli came near one of them he felt, he says, the deadly odour of a corpse. With many arts, the duke got them to meet him at Sinigaglia. He received their greetings cordially, pressed their hands, and gave them the accolade. They all rode into the town together, talking of military things. Cæsar courteously invited them to enter the palace, then quitted them, and they were immediately seized. 'I doubt if they will be alive to-morrow morning,' the Florentine secretary wrote without emotion to his government. They went through some form of trial, and before daybreak two of them were strangled, and two others shared the same fate as soon as Cæsar knew that the Pope had carried out his plans for making away by poison with the Cardinal who headed the rebellious faction at Rome.

Let us pause for a moment. One of the victims of Sinigaglia was Oliverotto da Fermo. His story is told in the eighth chapter of the *Prince*. He had been brought up from childhood by an uncle; he went out into the world to learn military service; in course of time, one day he wrote to his uncle at Fermo that he should like once more to see him and his paternal city, and, by way of showing his good compatriots that he had won some honour in life, he purposed to bring a hundred horsemen in his company. He came, and was honourably received. He invited his uncle and the chief men of Fermo to a feast, and when the feast was over, his soldiers sprang upon the guests and slew them all, and Oliverotto became the tyrant of the place. We may at any rate forgive Cæsar for, a year later, making sure work of Oliverotto. When his last hour came, he struggled to drive his dagger into the man with the cord. Here indeed were lions, foxes, catamounts.

This is obviously the key to Machiavelli's admiration for Borgia's policy. The men were all bandits together. Romagna is not and never was, said Dante two hundred years before, without war in the hearts of her tyrants (*Inf.* xxvii. 37). So it was now. It was full, says Machiavelli, of those who are called gentlemen, who live in idleness and abundance on the revenues of their estates, without any care of cultivating them, or of incurring any of the fatigue of getting a living; such men are pernicious anywhere, but most of all are those who are lords of castles, and have subjects who are under obedience to them. These lords, before the Pope and his terrible son took them in hand, were poor, yet had a mind to live as if they were rich, and so there was nothing for it, but rapine, extortion, and every other iniquity. Whether Cæsar and the Pope had wider designs than the reduction of these oppressors to order, we can never know. Machiavelli and most contemporaries thought that they had, but German historians of to-day differ. Probably the contemporaries knew best, but nothing can matter less.

We may as well finish Cæsar's story, because we never know until a man's end, whether the play has been tragedy or comedy. He seemed to be lord of the ascendant, when, in the summer after the transaction of Sinigaglia (1503), the Pope and he were one evening both stricken with malarious fever at Rome. There was talk of poison, but the better opinion seems to be that this is fable. Alexander VI. died; Cæsar, in the prime of his young man's strength, made a better fight for it, but when at last he recovered, his star had set. Machiavelli saw him and felt that Fortune this time had got the best of *virtù*. His subjects in the Romagna stood by him for a time, and then tyranny and disorder came back. The new Pope, Julius II., was not his friend, for though Cæsar had made the Spanish cardinals support his election, Julius had some old scores to pay, and as Machiavelli profoundly remarked, anybody who supposes that new services make great people forget old injuries, makes a vast mistake. So Cæsar found his way to Naples, with a safe conduct from Gonsalvo, the Great Captain. He reaped as he had sown. Once he had said, 'It is well to cheat those, who have been masters of treachery.' He now felt the force of his maxim. At Naples he was cordially received by Gonsalvo, dined often at his table, talked over all his plans, and suddenly one night as he was about to pass the postern, in spite of the safe conduct, an officer demanded his sword in the name of the King of Castile. To Spain he was sent. For some three years he went through strange and obscure adventures, fighting fortune with the aid of his indwelling demon to the very last. He was struck down in a fight at Viana in Navarre (1507), after a furious resistance; was stripped of his fine armour by men who did not know who he was; and his body was left naked, bloody, and riddled with wounds, on the ground. He was only thirty-one. His father, who was quite as desperate an evil-doer, died in his bed at seventy-two. So history cannot safely draw a moral.

From this digression let us return to mark some of the problems that Machiavelli raises. In one sense, we are shocked by his maxims in proportion to our forgetfulness of history. There have been, it is said, only two perfect princes in the world—Marcus Aurelius and Louis IX. of France. If you add to princes, presidents and prime ministers, the percentage might still be low. Among the canonised saints of the Roman Church, there have only been a dozen kings in eight centuries, and no more than four popes in the same period. So hard has it been 'to govern the world by paternosters.' It is well to take care lest in blaming Machiavelli for openly prescribing hypocrisy, men do not slip unperceived into something like hypocrisy of their own.

Take the subordination of religious creed to policy. In the age that immediately followed Machiavelli, three commanding figures stand out, and are cherished in the memories of men—William the Silent, Henry of Navarre, and Elizabeth of England. It needs no peevish or pharisaic memory to trace even in these imposing personages some of the lineaments of Machiavelli's hated and scandalous picture. William the Silent changed from Lutheran to Catholic, then back to Lutheran, and then from Lutheran to Calvinist. His numerous children were sometimes baptized in one of the three communions, sometimes in the other, just as political convenience served. Henry of Navarre abjured his Huguenot faith, then he returned to it, then he abjured it again. Our great Elizabeth, of famous memory, notoriously walked in tortuous and slippery paths. Again, the most dolorous chapter in all history is that which recounts how men and women were burned, hanged, shot, and tormented for heresy; and there is a considerable body of authors, who through the sixteenth and seventeenth centuries used against heretics Machiavelli's arguments for making short work with rebels, and asked with logical force why their reason of Church was not as good as his reason of State. In fact, how many of the wars of faith, from Monophysite, Arian, Iconoclast, downwards, have been at bottom far less concerned with opinion than with conflicts of race, nationality, and policy, and have been conducted on maxims of policy?

Frederick the Great is the hero of the most picturesque of modern historians. That strong ruler, as we all know, took it into his head to write a refutation of the *Prince*. 'Sir,' said Voltaire, 'I believe the very first advice that Machiavelli would have given to a disciple, would have been that he should write a refutation of his book.' Carlyle contemptuously regrets that his hero should have taken any trouble about the Italian's 'perverse little book,' and its incredible sophistries; pity he was not refuted by a kick from old Frederick William's jackboot; he deserved no more. Carlyle does not let us forget that nobody so quickly turns cynic as your high-flying transcendentalist, just as nobody takes wickedness so easily as the Antinomian who holds the highest doctrine about the incorruptibility of the spiritual nature. The plain truth is that Frederick, alike on his good side and his bad side, alike as the wise law-maker, the thrifty steward, the capable soldier, and as the robber of Silesia, and a leading accomplice, if not the inspirer, of the partition of Poland, was the aptest of all modern types of the perverse book. It was reserved for this century to see even that type depraved and distorted.

The most imposing of all incarnations of the doctrine that reason of State covers all, is Napoleon. Tacitus, said Napoleon, writes romances, Gibbon is no better than a man of sounding words, Machiavelli is the only one of them worth reading. No wonder that he thought so. All those maxims that have most scandalised mankind in the Italian writer of the sixteenth century, were the daily bread of the Italian soldier who planted his iron heel on the neck of Europe in the nineteenth. Yet Machiavelli at least sets decent limits and

45

conditions: the ruler may under compulsion be driven to set at nought pity, humanity, faith, religion, for the sake of the State, but though he should know how to enter upon evil when compelled, he should never turn from what is good when he can avoid it. Napoleon, a Cæsar Borgia on a giant scale, deliberately called evil good and good evil; and, almost alone among the past masters of all the arts of violence and fraud, he sacrificed pity, humanity, faith, religion, and public law, less for the sake of the State than to satisfy his own ravening egotism and exorbitant passion for personal domination. Napoleon, Charles IX., the Committee of Public Safety, would all have justified themselves by reason of State, and the Bartholomew massacre, the September massacres, and the murder of the Duc d'Enghien, only show what reason of State may come to in any age, in the hands of the practical logician with a knife in his grasp.

Turn from the Absolutist camp to the Republican. Mazzini is in some respects the loftiest moral genius of the century, and he said that though he did not approve the theory of the dagger, nay he deplored it, yet he had not the heart to curse the fact of the dagger. 'When a man,' he says, 'seeks by every possible artifice to betray an old friend to the police of the Foreign Ruler, and then a working man arises and slays the Judas in the broad daylight in the public streets—I have not the courage to cast

46

the first stone at one who thus takes upon himself to represent social justice and the abhorrence of tyranny,'

Even in modern democracy, many a secret spring works under decorous mechanism, and recalls Machiavelli's precept to keep the name and take away the thing. An eminent man endowed with remarkable compass of mind, not many years ago a professor in this university, imagined a modern writer, with the unflinching perspicacity of Machiavelli, analysing the party leader as the Italian analysed the tyrant or the prince. Such a writer, he said, would find that the party leader, though possessed of every sort of private virtue, yet is debarred by his position from the full practice of the great virtues of veracity, justice, and moral intrepidity; he can seldom tell the full truth; can never be fair to anybody but his followers and his associates; can rarely be bold except in the interests of his faction. The hint is ingenious and it may perhaps be salutary, but one must not overdo it. Party government is not the Reign of the Saints, but we should not be in a hurry to let the misgivings of political valetudinarianism persuade us that there is not at least as good a stock of veracity, justice, and moral intrepidity inside the world of parliaments or congress, as there is in the world without. But these three or four historic instances may serve to illustrate the ἀπορίαι, or awkward points, that Machiavelli's writings have propounded, for men capable of political reflection, in Europe for many generations past.

If one were to try to put the case for the Machiavellian philosophy in a modern way, it would, I suppose, be something of this kind:— Nature does not work by moral rules. Nature, 'red in tooth and claw,' does by system all that good men by system avoid. Is not the whole universe of sentient being haunted all day and all night long by the haggard shapes of Hunger, Cruelty, Force, Fear?

War again is not conducted by moral rules. To declare war is to suspend not merely *habeas corpus* but the Ten Commandments, and some other good commandments besides. A military manual, by an illustrious hand of our own day, warns us: 'As a nation we are brought up to feel it a disgrace even to succeed by falsehood. We keep hammering along with the conviction that honesty is the best policy, and that truth always wins in the long run. These sentiments do well for a copy-book, but a man who acts upon them had better sheath his sword forever.' One reason among others why we should keep the sword sheathed as long as we can.

Why should the ruler of a State be bound by a moral code from which the soldier is free? Why should not he have the benefit of what has been called the 'evolutionary beatitude,'—Blessed are the strong, for they shall prey on the weak? Right and wrong, cause and effect, are two sides of one question. 'Morality is the nature of things.' We must include in the computation the whole sum of consequences, and consider acts of State as worked out to their furthest results. Bishop Butler tells you that we cannot give the whole account of any one thing whatever, of all its causes, ends, and necessary adjuncts. In short, means and end are a single transaction. You must regard policy as a whole. The ruler as an individual is, like other men, 'no more than the generation of leaves, fleeting, a shadow, a dream.' But the State lives on after he has vanished. He is a trustee for times to come. He is not shaping his own life only, but guiding the long fortunes of a nation. Leaves fall, the tree stands.

Such is the defence of reason of State, of the worship of nation and empire. Everything that policy requires, justice sanctions. There are no crimes in politics, only blunders. 'The man of action is essentially conscienceless' (*Goethe*). 'Praised be those,' said one, in words much applauded by Machiavelli, 'who love their country rather than the safety of their souls.' 'Let us be Venetians first,' said Father Paul, 'and Christians after.'

We see now the deep questions that lie behind these sophistries, and all the alarming propositions in which they close. Does morality apply only to end and not to means? Is the State means or end? What does it really exist for? For the sake of the individual, his moral and material well-being, or is the individual a mere cog or pinion in the vast machine? How far is it true that citizenship dominates all other relations and duties, and is the most important of them? Are we to test the true civilisation of a State by anything else than the predominance of justice, right, equality, in its laws, its institutions, its relations to neighbours? Is one of the most important aspects of national policy its reaction upon the character of the nation itself, and can States enter on courses of duplicity and selfish violence, without paying the penalty in national demoralisation? What are we to think of such sayings as d'Alembert's motto for a virtuous man, 'I prefer my family to myself, my country to my family, and humanity to my country'? Is this the true order? To Machiavelli all these questions would have been futile. Yet the world, in spite of a thousand mischances, and at tortoise-pace, has steadily moved away from him and his Romans.

The modern conception of a State has long made it a moral person, capable of right and wrong, just as are the individuals composing it. Civilisation is taken to advance, exactly in proportion as communities leave behind them the violences of external nature, and of man in a state of war. The usages of war are constantly undergoing mitigation. Diplomacy, though it is said even now not to be wholly purged of lying, fraud, and duplicity, still is conscious of having a character to keep up for truth and plain dealing, so far as circumstances allow.

Such conferences, again, as those at Berlin and Brussels in our own day, imperfectly as they have worked, mark the recognition of duty towards inferior races. All these improvements in the character of nations were in the minds of the best men in Machiavelli's day. Reason of State has always been a plea for impeding and resisting them. Las Casas and other churchmen, Machiavelli's contemporaries, fought nobly at the Spanish court against the inhuman treatment of Indians in the New World, and they were defeated by arguments which read like maxims from the *Prince*. Grotius had fore-runners in his powerful contribution towards assuaging the abominations of war, but both letter and spirit in Machiavelli made all the other way. Times have come and gone since Machiavelli wrote down his deep truths, but in the great cycles of human change he can have no place among the strong thinkers, and orators, and writers, who have elevated the conception of the State, and humanised the methods and maxims of government, and raised citizenship to be 'a partnership in every virtue and in all perfection.' He turned to the past, just as scholars, architects, sculptors, turned to it, but the idea of reconstructing a society that had once been saturated with the great ruling conceptions of the thirteenth century, by trying to awaken the social energy of ancient Rome, was as much of an anachronism as Julian the Apostate.

Machiavelli has been supposed to put aside the question of right and wrong, just as the political economist or the analytical jurist used to do. Truly has it been said that the practical value of all sciences founded on abstractions, depends on the relative importance of the elements rejected, and the elements retained, in the process of abstraction. The view that he rejected moral elements of government for a scientific purpose and as a hypothetical postulate, seems highly doubtful. Is he not more intelligible, if we take him as following up the divorce of politics from theology, by a divorce from ethics also? He was laying down some maxims of government as an art; the end of that art is the security and permanence of the ruling power; and the fundamental principle from which he silently started, without any doubt or misgiving as to its soundness, was that the application of moral standards to this business, is as little to the point as it would be in the navigation of a ship.

The effect was fatal even for his own purpose, for what he put aside, whether for the sake of argument or because he thought them in substance irrelevant, were nothing less than the living forces by which societies subsist and governments are strong. A remarkable illustration occurred in his own century. Three or four years before all this on secular and ecclesiastical princedoms was written, John Calvin was born (1509). Calvin, with a union of fervid religious instinct and profound political genius, almost unexampled in European history, did in fact what Machiavelli tried to do on paper; he actually created a self-governed state, ruled it, defended it, maintained it, and made that little corner of Europe both the centre of a movement that shook France, England, Scotland, America, for long days to come, and at the same time he set up a bulwark against all the forces of Spanish and Roman reaction, in the pressing struggles of his own immediate day. Florence, Geneva, Holland, hold as high a place as the greatest States of Europe in the development of modern civilisation; but anybody with a turn for ingenious and idle speculation might ask himself whether, if the influence of Florence on European culture had never existed, the loss to mankind would have been as deep as if the little republic of Geneva had been wiped out by the dukes of Savoy. The unarmed prophet, said Machiavelli, thinking of Savonarola, is always sure to be destroyed, and his institutions to come to nought. If Machiavelli had been at Jerusalem two thousand years ago, he would have found nobody of any importance in his eyes, save Pontius Pilate and the Roman legionaries. He forgot the potent arms of moral force, and it was with these that, in the main, Calvin fought his victorious battle. We should not, it is quite true, forget that Calvin never for an instant scrupled to act on some of those very Italian maxims, which have been counted most hateful. He was as ready to resort to carnal weapons as other people. In spite of all the sophistries of sectarian apologists, Calvin's vindictive persecution of political opponents, and his share in the crime of burning Servetus, can only be justified on principles that are much the same as, and certainly not any better than, those prescribed for the tyrant in the *Prince*. Still the republic of Geneva was the triumph of moral force.

In Italy Savonarola had attempted a similar achievement. It was the last effort to reconcile the spirit of the new age to the old faith, but Italy was for a second time in her history in the desperate case of being able to endure *nec vitia nec remedia*, neither ills nor cure. In a curious passage (*Disc.*, iii. l), Machiavelli describes how Dominic and Francis in older days kindled afresh an expiring flame. He may have perceived that for Italy in this direction all was over. But if moral force and spiritual force is exhausted, with what hope are you to look for either good soldiers or good rulers?

The sixteenth century in Italy in some respects resembles the eighteenth in France. In both, old faiths were assailed, and new lamps were kindled. But the eighteenth century was a time of belief in the better elements of mankind. An illusion, you may say. Was it a worse illusion than disbelief in mankind? Machiavelli and his school saw only cunning, jealousy, perfidy, ingratitude, dupery, and yet on such a foundation as this they dreamed that they could build. What idealist or doctrinaire ever fell into a stranger error? Surrounded by the ruins of Italian nationality, says a writer of genius, 'he organises the abstract theory of the country with all the energy of the Committee of Public Safety, supported on the passion of twenty-five millions of Frenchmen. He carries in him the genius of the Convention. His theories strike like acts' (Quinet). But energy as an abstract theory is a bubble.

It is true to say that Machiavelli represents certain living forces in our actual world; that Science, with its survival of the fittest, unconsciously lends him illegitimate aid; that 'he is not a vanishing type, but a constant and contemporary influence' (*Acton*). This is because energy, force, will, violence, still keep alive in the world their resistance to the control of justice and conscience, humanity and right. In so far as he represents one side in that eternal struggle, and suggests one set of considerations about about it, he retains a place in the literature of modern political systems and of European morals.

Machiavelli : the zealous republican[2]

It is notorious that Machiavelli was, through life, a zealous republican. In the same year in which he composed his manual of King-craft, he suffered imprisonment and torture in the cause of public liberty. It seems inconceivable that the martyr of freedom should have designedly acted as the apostle of tyranny. Several eminent writers have, therefore, endeavoured to detect in this unfortunate performance some concealed meaning, more consistent with the character and conduct of the author than that which appears at the first glance.

One hypothesis is that Machiavelli intended to practise on the young Lorenzo de Medici a fraud similar to that which Sunderland is said to have employed against our James the Second, and that he urged his pupil to violent and perfidious measures, as the surest means of accelerating the moment of deliverance and revenge. Another supposition which Lord Bacon seems to countenance, is that the treatise was merely a piece of grave irony, intended to warn nations against the arts of ambitious men. It would be easy to show that neither of these solutions is consistent with many passages in The

---

[2] By Thomas B. Macaulay

Prince itself. But the most decisive refutation is that which is furnished by the other works of Machiavelli. In all the writings which he gave to the public, and in all those which the research of editors has, in the course of three centuries, discovered, in his Comedies, designed for the entertainment of the multitude, in his Comments on Livy, intended for the perusal of the most enthusiastic patriots of Florence, in his History, inscribed to one of the most amiable and estimable of the Popes, in his public despatches, in his private memoranda, the same obliquity of moral principle for which The Prince is so severely censured is more or less discernible. We doubt whether it would be possible to find, in all the many volumes of his compositions, a single expression indicating that dissimulation and treachery had ever struck him as discreditable.

After this, it may seem ridiculous to say that we are acquainted with few writings which exhibit so much elevation of sentiment, so pure and warm a zeal for the public good, or so just a view of the duties and rights of citizens, as those of Machiavelli. Yet so it is. And even from The Prince itself we could select many passages in support of this remark. To a reader of our age and country this inconsistency is, at first, perfectly bewildering. The whole man seems to be an enigma, a grotesque assemblage of incongruous qualities, selfishness and generosity, cruelty and benevolence, craft and simplicity, abject villainy and romantic heroism. One sentence is such as a veteran diplomatist would scarcely write in cipher for the direction of his most confidential spy; the next seems to be extracted from a theme composed by an ardent schoolboy on the death of Leonidas. An act of dexterous perfidy, and an act of patriotic self-devotion, call forth the same kind and the same degree of respectful admiration. The moral sensibility of the writer seems at once to be morbidly obtuse and morbidly acute. Two characters altogether dissimilar are united in him. They are not merely joined, but interwoven. They are the warp and the woof of his mind; and their combination, like that of the variegated threads in shot silk, gives to the whole texture a glancing and ever-changing appearance. The explanation might have been easy, if he had been a very weak or a very affected man. But he was evidently neither the one nor the other. His works prove, beyond all contradiction, that his understanding was strong, his taste pure, and his sense of the ridiculous exquisitely keen.

This is strange: and yet the strangest is behind. There is no reason whatever to think, that those amongst whom he lived saw anything shocking or incongruous in his writings. Abundant proofs remain of the high estimation in which both his works and his person were held by the most respectable among his contemporaries. Clement the Seventh patronised the publication of those very books which the Council of Trent, in the following generation, pronounced unfit for the perusal of Christians. Some members of the democratical party censured the Secretary for dedicating The Prince to a patron who bore the unpopular name of Medici. But to those immoral doctrines which have since called forth such severe reprehensions no exception appears to have been taken. The cry against them was first raised beyond the Alps, and seems to have been heard with amazement in Italy. The earliest assailant, as far as we are aware, was a countryman of our own, Cardinal Pole. The author of the Anti-Machiavelli was a French Protestant.

It is, therefore, in the state of moral feeling among the Italians of those times that we must seek for the real explanation of what seems most mysterious in the life and writings of this remarkable man. As this is a subject which suggests many interesting considerations, both political and metaphysical, we shall make no apology for discussing it at some length.

During the gloomy and disastrous centuries which followed the downfall of the Roman Empire, Italy had preserved, in a far greater degree than any other part of Western Europe, the traces of ancient civilisation. The night which descended upon her was the night of an Arctic summer. The dawn began to reappear before the last reflection of the preceding sunset had faded from the horizon. It was in the time of the French Merovingians and of the

Saxon Heptarchy that ignorance and ferocity seemed to have done their worst. Yet even then the Neapolitan provinces, recognising the authority of the Eastern Empire, preserved something of Eastern knowledge and refinement. Rome, protected by the sacred character of her Pontiffs, enjoyed at least comparative security and repose, Even in those regions where the sanguinary Lombards had fixed their monarchy, there was incomparably more of wealth, of information, of physical comfort, and of social order, than could be found in Gaul, Britain, or Germany.

That which most distinguished Italy from the neighbouring countries was the importance which the population of the towns, at a very early period, began to acquire. Some cities had been founded in wild and remote situations, by fugitives who had escaped from the rage of the barbarians. Such were Venice and Genoa, which preserved their freedom by their obscurity, till they became able to preserve it by their power. Other cities seem to have retained, under all the changing dynasties of invaders, under Odoacer and Theodoric, Narses and Alboin, the municipal institutions which had been conferred on them by the liberal policy of the Great Republic. In provinces which the central government was too feeble either to protect or to oppress, these institutions gradually acquired stability and vigour. The citizens, defended by their walls, and governed by their own magistrates and their own by-laws, enjoyed a considerable share of republican independence. Thus a strong democratic spirit was called into action. The Carlovingian sovereigns were too imbecile to subdue it. The generous policy of Otho encouraged it. It might perhaps have been suppressed by a close coalition between the Church and the Empire. It was fostered and invigorated by their disputes. In the twelfth century it attained its full vigour, and, after a long and doubtful conflict, triumphed over the abilities and courage of the Swabian princes.

The assistance of the Ecclesiastical power had greatly contributed to the success of the Guelfs. That success would, however, have been a doubtful good, if its only effect had been to substitute a moral for a political servitude, and to exalt the Popes at the expense of the Caesars. Happily the public mind of Italy had long contained the seeds of free opinions, which were now rapidly developed by the genial influence of free institutions. The people of that country had observed the whole machinery of the Church, its saints and its miracles, its lofty pretensions and its splendid ceremonial, its worthless blessings and its harmless curses, too long and too closely to be duped. They stood behind the scenes on which others were gazing with childish awe and interest. They witnessed the arrangement of the pulleys, and the manufacture of the thunders. They saw the natural faces and heard the natural voices of the actors. Distant nations looked on the Pope as the Vicegerent of the Almighty, the oracle of the All-wise, the umpire from whose decisions, in the disputes either of theologians or of kings, no Christian ought to appeal. The Italians were acquainted with all the follies of his youth, and with all the dishonest arts by which he had attained power. They knew how often he had employed the keys of the Church to release himself from the most sacred engagements, and its wealth to pamper his mistresses and nephews. The doctrines and rites of the established religion they treated with decent reverence. But though they still called themselves Catholics, they had ceased to be Papists. Those spiritual arms which carried terror into the palaces and camps of the proudest sovereigns excited only contempt in the immediate neighbourhood of the Vatican. Alexander, when he commanded our Henry the Second to submit to the lash before the tomb of a rebellious subject, was himself an exile. The Romans apprehending that he entertained designs against their liberties, had driven him from their city; and though he solemnly promised to confine himself for the future to his spiritual functions, they still refused to readmit him.

In every other part of Europe, a large and powerful privileged class trampled on the people and defied the Government. But in the most flourishing parts of Italy, the feudal nobles were reduced to comparative insignificance. In some districts they took shelter under the protection of the powerful commonwealths which they were unable to oppose, and gradually sank into the mass of burghers. In other places they possessed great influence; but it was an influence widely different from that which was exercised by the aristocracy of any Transalpine kingdom. They were not petty princes, but eminent citizens. Instead of strengthening their fastnesses among the mountains, they embellished their palaces in the market-place. The state of society in the Neapolitan dominions, and in some parts of the Ecclesiastical State, more nearly resembled that which existed in the great monarchies of Europe. But the Governments of Lombardy and Tuscany, through all their revolutions, preserved a different character. A people, when assembled in a town, is far more formidable to its rulers than when dispersed over a wide extent of country. The most arbitrary of the Caesars found it necessary to feed and divert the inhabitants of their unwieldy capital at the expense of the provinces. The citizens of Madrid have more than once besieged their sovereign in his own palace, and extorted from him the most humiliating concessions. The Sultans have often been compelled to propitiate the furious rabble of Constantinople with the head of an unpopular Vizier. From the same cause there was a certain tinge of democracy in the monarchies and aristocracies of Northern Italy.

Thus liberty, partially indeed and transiently, revisited Italy; and with liberty came commerce and empire, science and taste, all the comforts and all the ornaments of life. The Crusades, from which the inhabitants of other countries gained nothing but relics and wounds, brought to the rising commonwealths of the Adriatic and Tyrrhene seas a large increase of wealth, dominion, and knowledge. The moral and geographical position of those commonwealths enabled them to profit alike by the barbarism of the West and by the civilisation of the East. Italian ships covered every sea. Italian factories rose on every shore. The tables of Italian moneychangers were set in every city. Manufactures flourished. Banks were established. The operations of the commercial machine were facilitated by many useful and beautiful inventions. We doubt whether any country of Europe, our own excepted, have at the present time reached so high a point of wealth and civilisation as some parts of Italy had attained four hundred years ago. Historians rarely descend to those details from which alone the real state of a community can be collected. Hence posterity is too often deceived by the vague hyperboles of poets and rhetoricians, who mistake the splendour of a court for the happiness of a people. Fortunately, John Villani has given us an ample and precise account of the state of Florence in the early part of the fourteenth century. The revenue of the Republic amounted to three hundred thousand florins; a sum which, allowing for the depreciation of the precious metals, was at least equivalent to six hundred thousand pounds sterling; a larger sum than England and Ireland, two centuries ago, yielded annually to Elizabeth. The manufacture of wool alone employed two hundred factories and thirty thousand workmen. The cloth annually produced sold, at an average, for twelve hundred thousand florins; a sum fully equal in exchangeable value to two millions and a half of our money. Four hundred thousand florins were annually coined. Eighty banks conducted the commercial operations, not of Florence only but of all Europe. The transactions of these establishments were sometimes of a magnitude which may surprise even the contemporaries of the Barings and the Rothschilds. Two houses advanced to Edward the Third of England upwards of three hundred thousand marks, at a time when the mark contained more silver than fifty shillings of the present day, and when the value of silver was more than quadruple of what it now is. The city and its environs contained a hundred and seventy thousand inhabitants. In the various schools about ten thousand children were taught to read; twelve hundred studied arithmetic; six hundred received a learned education.

The progress of elegant literature and of the fine arts was proportioned to that of the public prosperity. Under the despotic successors of

Augustus, all the fields of intellect had been turned into arid wastes, still marked out by formal boundaries, still retaining the traces of old cultivation, but yielding neither flowers nor fruit. The deluge of barbarism came. It swept away all the landmarks. It obliterated all the signs of former tillage. But it fertilised while it devastated. When it receded, the wilderness was as the garden of God, rejoicing on every side, laughing, clapping its hands, pouring forth, in spontaneous abundance, everything brilliant, or fragrant, or nourishing. A new language, characterised by simple sweetness and simple energy, had attained perfection. No tongue ever furnished more gorgeous and vivid tints to poetry; nor was it long before a poet appeared who knew how to employ them. Early in the fourteenth century came forth the Divine Comedy, beyond comparison the greatest work of imagination which had appeared since the poems of Homer. The following generation produced indeed no second Dante: but it was eminently distinguished by general intellectual activity. The study of the Latin writers had never been wholly neglected in Italy. But Petrarch introduced a more profound, liberal, and elegant scholarship, and communicated to his countrymen that enthusiasm for the literature, the history, and the antiquities of Rome, which divided his own heart with a frigid mistress and a more frigid Muse. Boccaccio turned their attention to the more sublime and graceful models of Greece.

From this time, the admiration of learning and genius became almost an idolatry among the people of Italy. Kings and republics, cardinals and doges, vied with each other in honouring and flattering Petrarch. Embassies from rival States solicited the honour of his instructions. His coronation agitated the Court of Naples and the people of Rome as much as the most important political transaction could have done. To collect books and antiques, to found professorships, to patronise men of learning, became almost universal fashions among the great. The spirit of literary research allied itself to that of commercial enterprise. Every place to which the merchant princes of Florence extended their gigantic traffic, from the bazars of the Tigris to the monasteries of the Clyde, was ransacked for medals and manuscripts. Architecture, painting, and sculpture, were munificently encouraged. Indeed it would be difficult to name an Italian of eminence, during the period of which we speak, who, whatever may have been his general character, did not at least affect a love of letters and of the arts.

Knowledge and public prosperity continued to advance together. Both attained their meridian in the age of Lorenzo the Magnificent. We cannot refrain from quoting the splendid passage, in which the Tuscan Thucydides describes the state of Italy at that period. "Ridotta tutta in somma pace e tranquillita, coltivata non meno ne' luoghi piu montuosi e piu sterili che nelle pianure e regioni piu fertili, ne sottoposta ad altro imperio che de' suoi medesimi, non solo era abbondantissima d' abitatori e di ricchezze; ma illustrata sommamente dalla magnificenza di molti principi, dallo splendore di molte nobilissime e bellissime citta, dalla sedia e maesta della religione, fioriva d' uomini prestantissimi nell' amministrazione delle cose pubbliche, e d'ingegni molto nobili in tutte le scienze, ed in qualunque arte preclara ed industriosa." When we peruse this just and splendid description, we can scarcely persuade ourselves that we are reading of times in which the annals of England and France present us only with a frightful spectacle of poverty, barbarity, and ignorance. From the oppressions of illiterate masters, and the sufferings of a degraded peasantry, it is delightful to turn to the opulent and enlightened States of Italy, to the vast and magnificent cities, the ports, the arsenals, the villas, the museums, the libraries, the marts filled with every article of comfort or luxury, the factories swarming with artisans, the Apennines covered with rich cultivation up to their very summits, the Po wafting the harvests of Lombardy to the granaries of Venice, and carrying back the silks of Bengal and the furs of Siberia to the palaces of Milan. With peculiar pleasure, every cultivated mind must repose on the fair, the happy, the glorious Florence, the halls which rang with the mirth of Pulci, the cell where twinkled the midnight lamp of Politian, the statues on which the young eye of Michael Angelo glared with the frenzy of a kindred inspiration, the gardens in which Lorenzo meditated some sparkling song for the May-day dance of the Etrurian virgins. Alas for the beautiful city! Alas for the wit and the learning, the genius and the love!

A time was at hand, when all the seven vials of the Apocalypse were to be poured forth and shaken out over those pleasant countries, a time of slaughter, famine, beggary, infamy, slavery, despair.

In the Italian States, as in many natural bodies, untimely decrepitude was the penalty of precocious maturity. Their early greatness, and their early decline, are principally to be attributed to the same cause, the preponderance which the towns acquired in the political system.

In a community of hunters or of shepherds, every man easily and necessarily becomes a soldier. His ordinary avocations are perfectly compatible with all the duties of military service. However remote may be the expedition on which he is bound, he finds it easy to transport with him the stock from which he derives his subsistence. The whole people is an army; the whole year a march.

Such was the state of society which facilitated the gigantic conquests of Attila and Tamerlane.

But a people which subsists by the cultivation of the earth is in a very different situation. The husbandman is bound to the soil on which he labours. A long campaign would be ruinous to him. Still his pursuits are such as give to his frame both the active and the passive strength necessary to a soldier. Nor do they, at least in the infancy of agricultural science, demand his uninterrupted attention. At particular times of the year he is almost wholly unemployed, and can, without injury to himself, afford the time necessary for a short expedition. Thus the legions of Rome were supplied during its earlier wars. The season during which the fields did not require the presence of the cultivators sufficed for a short inroad and a battle. These operations, too frequently interrupted to produce decisive results, yet served to keep up among the people a degree of discipline and courage which rendered them, not only secure, but formidable. The archers and billmen of the middle ages, who, with provisions for forty days at their backs, left the fields for the camp, were troops of the same description.

But when commerce and manufactures begin to flourish a great change takes place. The sedentary habits of the desk and the loom render the exertions and hardships of war insupportable. The business of traders and artisans requires their constant presence

71

and attention. In such a community there is little superfluous time; but there is generally much superfluous money. Some members of the society are, therefore, hired to relieve the rest from a task inconsistent with their habits and engagements.

The history of Greece is, in this, as in many other respects, the best commentary on the history of Italy. Five hundred years before the Christian era, the citizens of the republics round the Aegean Sea formed perhaps the finest militia that ever existed. As wealth and refinement advanced, the system underwent a gradual alteration. The Ionian States were the first in which commerce and the arts were cultivated, and the first in which the ancient discipline decayed. Within eighty years after the battle of Plataea, mercenary troops were everywhere plying for battles and sieges. In the time of Demosthenes, it was scarcely possible to persuade or compel the Athenians to enlist for foreign service. The laws of Lycurgus prohibited trade and manufactures. The Spartans, therefore, continued to form a national force long after their neighbours had begun to hire soldiers. But their military spirit declined with their singular institutions. In the second century before Christ, Greece contained only one nation of warriors, the savage highlanders of Aetolia, who were some generations behind their countrymen in civilisation and intelligence.

All the causes which produced these effects among the Greeks acted still more strongly on the modern Italians. Instead of a power like Sparta, in its nature warlike, they had amongst them an ecclesiastical state, in its nature pacific. Where there are numerous slaves, every freeman is induced by the strongest motives to familiarise himself with the use of arms. The commonwealths of Italy did not, like those of Greece, swarm with thousands of these household enemies. Lastly, the mode in which military operations were conducted during the prosperous times of Italy was peculiarly unfavourable to the formation of an efficient militia. Men covered with iron from head to foot, armed with ponderous lances, and mounted on horses of the largest breed, were considered as composing the strength of an army. The infantry was regarded as comparatively worthless, and was neglected till it became really so. These tactics maintained their ground for centuries in most parts of Europe. That foot- soldiers could withstand the charge of heavy cavalry was thought utterly impossible, till, towards the close of the fifteenth century, the rude mountaineers of Switzerland dissolved the spell, and astounded the most experienced generals by receiving the dreaded shock on an impenetrable forest of pikes.

The use of the Grecian spear, the Roman sword, or the modern bayonet, might be acquired with comparative ease. But nothing short of the daily exercise of years could train the man-at-arms to support his ponderous panoply, and manage his unwieldy weapon. Throughout Europe this most important branch of war became a separate profession. Beyond the Alps, indeed, though a profession, it was not generally a trade. It was the duty and the amusement of a large class of country gentlemen. It was the service by which they held their lands, and the diversion by which, in the absence of mental resources, they beguiled their leisure. But in the Northern States of Italy, as we have already remarked, the growing power of the cities, where it had not exterminated this order of men, had completely changed their habits. Here, therefore, the practice of employing mercenaries became universal, at a time when it was almost unknown in other countries.

When war becomes the trade of a separate class, the least dangerous course left to a government is to force that class into a standing army. It is scarcely possible, that men can pass their lives in the service of one State, without feeling some interest in its greatness. Its victories are their victories. Its defeats are their defeats. The contract loses something of its mercantile character. The services of the soldier are considered as the effects of patriotic zeal, his pay as the tribute of national gratitude. To betray the power which employs him, to be even remiss in its service, are in his eyes the most atrocious and degrading of crimes.

When the princes and commonwealths of Italy began to use hired troops, their wisest course would have been to form separate military establishments. Unhappily this was not done. The mercenary warriors of the Peninsula, instead of being attached to the service of different powers, were regarded as the common property of all. The connection between the State and its defenders was reduced to the most simple and naked traffic. The adventurer brought his horse, his weapons, his strength, and his experience, into the market. Whether the King of Naples or the Duke of Milan, the Pope or the Signory of Florence, struck the bargain, was to him a matter of perfect indifference. He was for the highest wages and the longest term. When the campaign for which he had contracted was finished, there was neither law nor punctilio to prevent him from instantly turning his arms against his late masters. The soldier was altogether disjoined from the citizen and from the subject.

The natural consequences followed. Left to the conduct of men who neither loved those whom they defended, nor hated those whom they opposed, who were often bound by stronger ties to the army against which they fought than to the State which they served, who lost by the termination of the conflict, and gained by its prolongation, war completely changed its character. Every man came into the field of battle impressed with the knowledge that, in a few days, he might be taking the pay of the power against which he was then employed, and, fighting by the side of his enemies against his associates. The strongest interests and the strongest feelings concurred to mitigate the hostility of those who had lately been brethren in arms, and who might soon be brethren in arms once more. Their common profession was a bond of union not to be forgotten even when they were engaged in the service of contending parties. Hence it was that operations, languid and indecisive beyond any recorded in history, marches and counter-marches, pillaging expeditions and blockades, bloodless capitulations and equally bloodless combats, make up the military history of Italy during the course of nearly two centuries. Mighty armies fight from sunrise to sunset. A great victory is won. Thousands of prisoners are taken; and hardly a life is lost. A pitched battle seems to have been really less dangerous than an ordinary civil tumult.

Courage was now no longer necessary even to the military character. Men grew old in camps, and acquired the highest renown by their warlike achievements, without being once required to face serious danger. The political consequences are too well known. The richest and most enlightened part of the world was left undefended to the assaults of every barbarous invader, to the brutality of Switzerland, the insolence of France, and the fierce rapacity of Arragon. The moral effects which

76

followed from this state of things were still more remarkable.

Among the rude nations which lay beyond the Alps, valour was absolutely indispensable. Without it none could be eminent; few could be secure. Cowardice was, therefore, naturally considered as the foulest reproach. Among the polished Italians, enriched by commerce, governed by law, and passionately attached to literature, everything was done by superiority and intelligence. Their very wars, more pacific than the peace of their neighbours, required rather civil than military qualifications. Hence, while courage was the point of honour in other countries, ingenuity became the point of honour in Italy.

From these principles were deduced, by processes strictly analogous, two opposite systems of fashionable morality. Through the greater part of Europe, the vices which peculiarly belong to timid dispositions, and which are the natural defence Of weakness, fraud, and hypocrisy, have always been most disreputable. On the other hand, the excesses of haughty and daring spirits have been treated with indulgence, and even with respect. The Italians regarded with corresponding lenity those crimes which require self-command, address, quick observation, fertile invention, and profound knowledge of human nature.

Such a prince as our Henry the Fifth would have been the idol of the North. The follies of his youth, the selfish ambition of his manhood, the Lollards roasted at slow fires the prisoners massacred on the field of battle, the expiring lease of priestcraft renewed for another century, the dreadful legacy of a causeless and hopeless war bequeathed to a people who had no interest in its event, everything is forgotten but the victory of Agincourt. Francis Sforza, on the other hand, was the model of Italian heroes. He made his employers and his rivals alike his tools. He first overpowered his open enemies by the help of faithless allies; he then armed himself against his allies with the spoils taken from his enemies. By his incomparable dexterity, he raised himself from the precarious and dependent situation of a military adventurer to the first throne of Italy. To such a man much was forgiven, hollow friendship, ungenerous enmity, violated faith. Such are the opposite errors which men commit, when their morality is not a science but a taste, when they abandon eternal principles for accidental associations.

We have illustrated our meaning by an instance taken from history. We will select another from fiction. Othello murders his wife; he gives orders for the murder of his lieutenant; he ends by murdering himself. Yet he never loses the esteem and affection of Northern readers. His intrepid and ardent spirit redeems everything. The unsuspecting confidence with which he listens to his adviser, the agony with which he shrinks from the thought of shame, the tempest of passion with which he commits his crimes, and the haughty fearlessness with which he avows them, give an extraordinary interest to his character. Iago, on the contrary, is the object of universal loathing. Many are inclined to suspect that Shakspeare has been seduced into an exaggeration unusual with him, and has drawn a monster who has no archetype in human nature. Now we suspect that an Italian audience in the fifteenth century would have felt very differently. Othello would have inspired nothing but detestation and contempt. The folly with which he trusts the friendly professions of a man whose promotion he had obstructed, the credulity with which he takes unsupported assertions, and trivial circumstances, for unanswerable proofs, the violence with which he silences the exculpation till the exculpation can only aggravate his misery, would have excited the abhorrence and disgust of the spectators. The conduct of Iago they would assuredly have condemned; but they would have condemned it as we condemn that of his victim. Something of interest and respect would have mingled with their disapprobation. The readiness of the traitor's wit, the clearness of his judgment, the skill with which he penetrates the dispositions of others and conceals his own, would have ensured to him a certain portion of their esteem.

So wide was the difference between the Italians and their neighbours. A similar difference existed between the Greeks of the second century before Christ, and their masters the Romans. The conquerors, brave and resolute, faithful to their engagements, and strongly influenced by religious feelings, were, at the same time, ignorant, arbitrary, and cruel. With the vanquished people were deposited all the art, the science, and the literature of the Western world. In poetry, in philosophy, in painting, in architecture, in sculpture, they had no rivals. Their manners were polished, their perceptions acute, their invention ready; they were tolerant, affable, humane; but of courage and sincerity they were almost utterly destitute. Every rude centurion consoled himself for his intellectual inferiority, by remarking that knowledge and taste seemed only to make men atheists, cowards, and slaves. The distinction long continued to be strongly marked, and furnished an admirable subject for the fierce sarcasms of Juvenal.

The citizen of an Italian commonwealth was the Greek of the time of Juvenal and the Greek of the time of Pericles, joined in one. Like the former, he was timid and pliable, artful and mean. But, like the latter, he had a country. Its independence and prosperity were dear to him. If his character were degraded by some base crimes, it was, on the other hand, ennobled by public spirit and by an honourable ambition,

A vice sanctioned by the general opinion is merely a vice. The evil terminates in itself. A vice condemned by the general opinion produces a pernicious effect on the whole character. The former is a local malady, the latter a constitutional taint. When the reputation of the offender is lost, he too often flings the remains of his virtue after it in despair. The Highland gentleman who, a century ago, lived by taking blackmail from his neighbours, committed the same crime for which Wild was accompanied to Tyburn by the huzzas of two hundred thousand people. But there can be no doubt that he was a much less depraved man than Wild. The deed for which Mrs.Brownrigg was hanged sinks into nothing, when compared with theconduct of the Roman who treated the public to a hundred pair of gladiators. Yet we should greatly wrong such a Roman if we supposed that his disposition was as cruel as that of Mrs. Brownrigg. In our own country, a woman forfeits her place in society by what, in a man, is too commonly considered as an honourable distinction, and, at worst, as a venial error. The consequence is notorious. The moral principle of a woman is frequently more impaired by a single lapse from virtue than that of a man by twenty years of intrigues. Classical antiquity would furnish us with instances stronger, if possible, than those to which we have referred.

We must apply this principle to the case before us. Habits of dissimulation and falsehood, no doubt, mark a man of our age and country as utterly worthless and abandoned. But it by no means follows that a similar judgment would be just in the case of an Italian of the middle ages. On the contrary, we frequently find those faults which we are accustomed to consider as certain indications of a mind altogether depraved, in company with great and good qualities, with generosity, with benevolence, with disinterestedness. From such a state of society, Palamedes, in the admirable dialogue of Hume, might have drawn illustrations of his theory as striking as any of those with which Fourli furnished him. These are not, we well know, the lessons which historians are generally most careful to teach, or readers most willing to learn. But they are not therefore useless. How Philip disposed his troops at Chaeronea, where Hannibal crossed the Alps, whether Mary blew up Darnley, or Siquier shot Charles the Twelfth, and ten thousand other questions of the same description, are in themselves unimportant. The inquiry may amuse us, but the decision leaves us no wiser. He alone reads history aright who, observing how powerfully circumstances influence the feelings and opinions of men, how often vices pass into virtues and paradoxes into axioms, learns to distinguish what is accidental and transitory in human nature from what is essential and immutable.

In this respect no history suggests more important reflections than that of the Tuscan and

Lombard commonwealths. The character of the Italian statesman seems, at first sight, a collection of contradictions, a phantom as monstrous as the portress of hell in Milton, half divinity, half snake, majestic and beautiful above, grovelling and poisonous below, We see a man whose thoughts and words have no connection with each other, who never hesitates at an oath when he wishes to seduce, who never wants a pretext when he is inclined to betray. His cruelties spring, not from the heat of blood, or the insanity of uncontrolled power, but from deep and cool meditation. His passions, like well-trained troops, are impetuous by rule, and in their most headstrong fury never forget the discipline to which they have been accustomed. His whole soul is occupied with vast and complicated schemes of ambition: yet his aspect and language exhibit nothing but philosophical moderation. Hatred and revenge eat into his heart: yet every look is a cordial smile, every gesture a familiar caress. He never excites the suspicion of his adversaries by petty provocations. His purpose is disclosed only when it is accomplished. His face is unruffled, his speech is courteous, till vigilance is laid asleep, till a vital point is exposed, till a sure aim is taken; and then he strikes for the first and last time. Military courage, the boast of the sottish German, of the frivolous and prating Frenchman, of the romantic and arrogant Spaniard, he neither possesses nor values. He shuns danger, not because he is insensible to shame, but because, in the society in which he lives, timidity has ceased to be shameful. To do an injury openly is, in his estimation, as wicked as to do it secretly, and far less profitable. With him the most honourable means are those which are the surest, the speediest, and the darkest. He cannot comprehend how a man should scruple to deceive those whom he does not scruple to destroy. He would think it madness to declare open hostilities against rivals whom he might stab in a friendly embrace, or poison in a consecrated wafer.

Yet this man, black with the vices which we consider as most loathsome, traitor, hypocrite, coward, assassin, was by no means destitute even of those virtues which we generally consider as indicating superior elevation of character. In civil courage, in perseverance, in presence of mind, those barbarous warriors, who were foremost in the battle or the breach, were far his inferiors. Even the dangers which he avoided with a caution almost pusillanimous never confused his perceptions, never paralysed his inventive faculties, never wrung out one secret from his smooth tongue, and his inscrutable brow. Though a dangerous enemy, and a still more dangerous accomplice, he could be a just and beneficent ruler. With so much unfairness in his policy, there was an extraordinary degree of fairness in his intellect. Indifferent to truth in the transactions of life, he was honestly devoted to truth in the researches of speculation. Wanton cruelty was not in his nature. On the contrary, where no political object was at stake, his disposition was soft and humane. The susceptibility of his nerves and the activity of his imagination inclined him, to sympathise with the feelings of others, and to delight in the charities and courtesies of social life. Perpetually descending to actions which might seem to mark a mind diseased through all its faculties, he had nevertheless an exquisite sensibility, both for the natural and the moral sublime, for every graceful and every lofty conception. Habits of petty intrigue and dissimulation might have rendered him incapable of great general views, but that the expanding effect of his philosophical studies counteracted the narrowing tendency. He had the keenest enjoyment of wit, eloquence, and poetry. The fine arts profited alike by the severity of his judgment, and by the liberality of his patronage. The portraits of some of the remarkable Italians of those times are perfectly in harmony with this description. Ample and majestic foreheads, brows strong and dark, but not frowning, eyes of which the calm full gaze, while it expresses nothing, seems to discern everything, cheeks pale with thought and sedentary habits, lips formed with feminine delicacy, but compressed with more than masculine decision, mark out men at once enterprising and timid, men equally skilled in detecting the purposes of others, and in concealing their own, men who must have been formidable enemies and unsafe allies, but men, at the same time, whose tempers were mild and equable, and who possessed an amplitude and subtlety of intellect which would have rendered them eminent either in active or in contemplative life, and fitted them either to govern or to instruct mankind.

Every age and every nation has certain characteristic vices, which prevail almost universally, which scarcely any person scruples to avow, and which even rigid moralists but faintly censure. Succeeding generations change the fashion of their morals, with the fashion of their hats and their coaches; take some other kind of wickedness under their patronage, and wonder at the depravity of their ancestors. Nor is this all. Posterity, that high court of appeal which is never tired of eulogising its own justice and discernment, acts on such occasions like a Roman dictator after a general mutiny. Finding the delinquents too numerous to be all punished, it selects some of them at hazard, to bear the whole penalty of an offence in which they are not more deeply implicated than those who escape, Whether decimation be a convenient mode of military execution, we know not; but we solemnly protest against the introduction of such a principle into the philosophy of history.

In the present instance, the lot has fallen on Machiavelli, a man whose public conduct was upright and honourable, whose views of morality, where they differed from those of the persons around him, seemed to have differed for the better, and whose only fault was, that, having adopted some of the maxims then generally received, he arranged them more luminously, and expressed them more forcibiy, than any other writer.

Having now, we hope, in some degree cleared the personal character of Machiavelli, we come to the consideration of his works. As a poet he is not entitled to a high place; but his comedies deserve attention.

The Mandragola, in particular, is superior to the best of Goldoni, and inferior only to the best of Moliere. It is the work of a man who, if he had devoted himself to the drama, would probably have attained the highest eminence, and produced a permanent and salutary effect on the national taste. This we infer, not so much from the degree, as from the kind of its excellence. There are compositions which indicate still greater talent, and which are perused with still greater delight, from which we should have drawn very different conclusions. Books quite worthless are quite harmless. The sure sign of the general decline of an art is the frequent occurrence, not of deformity, but of misplaced beauty. In general, Tragedy is corrupted by eloquence, and Comedy by wit.

The real object of the drama is the exhibition of human character. This, we conceive, is no arbitrary canon, originating in local and temporary associations, like those canons which regulate the number of acts in a play, or of syllables in a line. To this fundamental law every other regulation is subordinate. The situations which most signally develop character form the best plot. The mother tongue of the passions is the best style.

This principle rightly understood, does not debar the poet from any grace of composition. There is no style in which some man may not under some circumstances express himself. There is therefore no style which the drama rejects, none which it does not occasionally require. It is in the discernment of place, of time, and of person, that the inferior artists fail. The fantastic rhapsody of Mercutio, the elaborate declamation of Antony, are, where Shakspeare has placed them, natural and pleasing. But Dryden would have made Mercutio challenge Tybalt in hyperboles as fanciful as those in which he describes the chariot of Mab. Corneille would have represented Antony as scolding and coaxing Cleopatra with all the measured rhetoric of a funeral oration.

No writers have injured the Comedy of England so deeply as Congreve and Sheridan. Both were men of splendid wit and polished taste. Unhappily, they made all their characters in their own likeness. Their works bear the same relation to the legitimate drama which a transparency bears to a painting. There are no delicate touches, no hues imperceptibly fading into each other: the whole is lighted up with an universal glare. Outlines and tints are forgotten in the common blaze which illuminates all. The flowers and fruits of the intellect abound; but it is the abundance of a jungle, not of a garden, unwholesome, bewildering, unprofitable from its very plenty rank from its very fragrance. Every fop, every boor, every valet, is a man of wit. The very butts and dupes, Tattle, Witwould, Puff, Acres, outshine the whole Hotel of Rambouillet. To prove the whole system of this school erroneous, it is only necessary to apply the test which dissolved the enchanted Florimel, to place the true by the false Thalia, to contrast the most celebrated characters which have been drawn by the writers of whom we speak with the Bastard in King John or the Nurse in Romeo and Juliet. It was not surely from want of wit that Shakspeare adopted so different a manner. Benedick and Beatrice throw Mirabel and Millamant into the shade. All the good sayings of the facetious houses of Absolute and Surface might have been clipped from the single character of Falstaff, without being missed. It would have been easy for that fertile mind to have given Bardolph and Shallow as much wit as Prince Hal, and to have made Dogberry and

Verges retort on each other in sparkling epigrams. But he knew that such indiscriminate prodigality was, to use his own admirable language, "from the purpose of playing, whose end, both at the first and now, was, and is, to hold, as it were, the mirror up to Nature."

This digression will enable our readers to understand what we mean when we say that in the Mandragola, Machiavelli has proved that he completely understood the nature of the dramatic art, and possessed talents which would have enabled him to excel in it. By the correct and vigorous delineation of human nature, it produces interest without a pleasing or skilful plot, and laughter without the least ambition of wit. The lover, not a very delicate or generous lover, and his adviser the parasite, are drawn with spirit. The hypocritical confessor is an admirable portrait. He is, if we mistake not, the original of Father Dominic, the best comic character of Dryden. But old Nicias is the glory of the piece. We cannot call to mind anything that resembles him. The follies which Moliere ridicules are those of affection, not those of fatuity. Coxcombs and pedants, not absolute simpletons, are his game. Shakspeare has indeed a vast assortment of fools; but the precise species of which we speak is not, if we remember right, to be found there. Shallow is a fool. But his animal spirits supply, to a certain degree, the place of cleverness. His talk is to that of Sir John what soda water is to champagne. It has the effervescence though not the body or the flavour. Slender and Sir Andrew Aguecheek are fools, troubled with an uneasy consciousness of their folly, which in the latter produces meekness and docility, and in the former, awkwardness, obstinacy, and confusion. Cloten is an arrogant fool, Osric a foppish fool, Ajax a savage fool; but Nicias is, as Thersites says of Patroclus, a fool positive. His mind is occupied by no strong feeling; it takes every character, and retains none; its aspect is diversified, not by passions, but by faint and transitory semblances of passion, a mock joy, a mock fear, a mock love, a mock pride, which chase each other like shadows over its surface, and vanish as soon as they appear. He is just idiot enough to be an object, not of pity or horror, but of ridicule. He bears some resemblance to poor Calandrino, whose mishaps, as recounted by Boccaccio, have made all Europe merry for more than four centuries. He perhaps resembles still more closely Simon da Villa, to whom Bruno and Buffalmacco promised the love of the Countess Civillari. Nicias is, like Simon, of a learned profession; and the dignity with which he wears the doctoral fur, renders his absurdities infinitely more grotesque. The old Tuscan is the very language for such a being. Its peculiar simplicity gives even to the most forcible reasoning and the most brilliant wit an infantine air, generally delightful, but to a foreign reader sometimes a little ludicrous. Heroes and statesmen seem to lisp when they use it. It becomes Nicias incomparably, and renders all his silliness infinitely more silly. We may add, that the verses with which the Mandragola is interspersed, appear to us to be the most spirited and correct of all that Machiavelli has written in metre. He seems to have entertained the same opinion; for he has introduced some of them in other places. The contemporaries of the author were not blind to the merits of this striking piece. It was acted at Florence with the greatest success. Leo the Tenth was among its admirers, and by his order it was represented at Rome.

[Nothing can be more evident than that Paulus Jovius designates the Mandragola under the name of the Nicias. We should not have noticed what is so perfectly obvious. were it not that this natural and palpable misnomer has led the sagacious and industrious Bayle into a gross error.]

The Clizia is an imitation of the Casina of Plautus, which is itself an imitation of the lost kleroumenoi of Diphilus. Plautus was, unquestionably, one of the best Latin writers; but the Casina is by no means one of his best plays; nor is it one which offers great facilities to an imitator. The story is as alien from modern habits of life, as the manner in which it is developed from the modern fashion of composition. The lover remains in the country and the heroine in her chamber during the whole action, leaving their fate to be decided by a foolish father, a cunning mother, and two knavish servants. Machiavelli has executed his task with judgment and taste. He has accommodated the plot to a different state of society, and has very dexterously connected it with the history of his own times. The relation of the trick put on the doting old lover is exquisitely humorous. It is far superior to the corresponding passage in the Latin comedy, and scarcely yields to the account which Falstaff gives of his ducking.

Two other comedies without titles, the one in prose, the other in verse, appear among the works of Machiavelli. The former is very short, lively enough, but of no great value. The latter we can scarcely believe to be genuine. Neither its merits nor its defects remind us of the reputed author. It was first printed in 1796, from a manuscript discovered in the celebrated library of the Strozzi. Its genuineness, if we have been rightly informed, is established solely by the comparison of hands. Our suspicions are strengthened by the circumstance, that the same manuscript contained a description of the plague of 1527, which has also, in consequence, been added to the works of Machiavelli. Of this last composition the strongest external evidence would scarcely induce us to believe him guilty. Nothing was ever written more detestable in matter and manner. The narrations, the reflections, the jokes, the lamentations, are all the very worst of their respective kinds, at once trite and affected, threadbare tinsel from the Rag Fairs and Monmouth Streets of literature. A foolish schoolboy might write such a piece, and, after he had written it, think it much finer than the incomparable introduction of the Decameron. But that a shrewd statesman, whose earliest works are characterised by manliness of thought and language, should, at near sixty years of age, descend to such puerility, is utterly inconceivable.

The little novel of Belphegor is pleasantly conceived and pleasantly told. But the extravagance of the satire in some measure injures its effect. Machiavelli was unhappily married; and his wish to avenge his own cause and that of his brethren in misfortune, carried him beyond even the licence of fiction. Jonson seems to have combined some hints taken from this tale, with others from Boccaccio, in the plot of The Devil is an Ass, a play which, though not the most highly finished of his compositions, is perhaps that which exhibits the strongest proofs of genius.

The Political Correspondence of Machiavelli, first published in 1767, is unquestionably genuine, and highly valuable. The unhappy circumstances in which his country was placed during the greater part of his public life gave extraordinary encouragement to diplomatic talents. From the moment that Charles the Eighth descended from the

Alps, the whole character of Italian politics was changed. The governments of the Peninsula ceased to form an independent system. Drawn from their old orbit by the attraction of the larger bodies which now approached them, they became mere satellites of France and Spain. All their disputes, internal and external, were decided by foreign influence. The contests of opposite factions were carried on, not as formerly in the senate- house or in the marketplace, but in the antechambers of Louis and Ferdinand. Under these circumstances, the prosperity of the Italian States depended far more on the ability of their foreign agents, than on the conduct of those who were intrusted with the domestic administration. The ambassador had to discharge functions far more delicate than transmitting orders of knighthood, introducing tourists, or presenting his brethren with the homage of his high consideration. He was an advocate to whose management the dearest interests of his clients were intrusted, a spy clothed with an inviolable character. Instead of consulting, by a reserved manner and ambiguous style, the dignity of those whom he represented, he was to plunge into all the intrigues of the Court at which he resided, to discover and flatter every weakness of the prince, and of the favourite who governed the prince, and of the lacquey who governed the favourite. He was to compliment the mistress and bribe the confessor, to panegyrise or supplicate, to laugh or weep, to accommodate himself to every caprice, to lull every suspicion, to treasure every hint, to be everything, to observe everything, to endure everything. High as the art of political intrigue had been carried in Italy, these were times which required it all.

On these arduous errands Machiavelli was frequently employed. He was sent to treat with the King of the Romans and with the Duke of Valentinois. He was twice ambassador of the Court of Rome, and thrice at that of France. In these missions, and in several others of inferior importance, he acquitted himself with great dexterity. His despatches form one of the most amusing and instructive collections extant. The narratives are clear and agreeably written; the remarks on men and things clever and judicious. The conversations are reported in a spirited and characteristic manner. We find ourselves introduced into the presence of the men who, during twenty eventful years, swayed the destinies of Europe. Their wit and their folly, their fretfulness and their merriment, are exposed to us. We are admitted to overhear their chat, and to watch their familiar gestures. It is interesting and curious to recognise, in circumstances which elude the notice of historians, the feeble violence and shallow cunning of Louis the Twelfth; the bustling insignificance of Maximilian, cursed with an impotent pruriency for renown, rash yet timid, obstinate yet fickle, always in a hurry, yet always too late; the fierce and haughty energy which gave dignity to the eccentricities of Julius; the soft and graceful manners which masked the insatiable ambition and the implacable hatred of Caesar Borgia.

We have mentioned Caesar Borgia. It is impossible not to pause for a moment on the name of a man in whom the political morality of Italy was so strongly personified, partially blended with the sterner lineaments of the Spanish character. On two important occasions Machiavelli was admitted to his society; once, at the moment when Caesar's splendid villainy achieved its most signal triumph, when he caught in one snare and crushed at one blow all his most formidable rivals; and again when, exhausted by disease and overwhelmed by misfortunes, which no human prudence could have averted, he was the prisoner of the deadliest enemy of his house. These interviews between the greatest speculative and the greatest practical statesman of the age are fully described in the Correspondence, and form perhaps the most interesting part of it.

From some passages in The Prince, and perhaps also from some indistinct traditions, several writers have supposed a connection between those remarkable men much closer than ever existed. The Envoy has even been accused of prompting the crimes of the artful and merciless tyrant. But from the official documents it is clear that their intercourse, though ostensibly amicable, was in reality hostile. It cannot be doubted, however, that the imagination of Machiavelli was strongly impressed, and his speculations on government coloured, by the observations which he made on the singular character and equally singular fortunes of a man who under such disadvantages had achieved such exploits; who, when sensuality, varied through innumerable forms, could no longer stimulate his sated mind, found a more powerful and durable excitement in the intense thirst of empire and revenge; who emerged from the sloth and luxury of the Roman purple the first prince and general of the age; who, trained in an unwarlike profession, formed a gallant army out of the dregs of an unwarlike people; who, after acquiring sovereignty by destroying his enemies, acquired popularity by destroying his tools; who had begun to employ for the most salutary ends the power which he had attained by the most atrocious means; who tolerated within the sphere of his iron despotism no plunderer or oppressor but himself; and who fell at last amidst the mingled curses and regrets of a people of whom his genius had been the wonder, and might have been the salvation. Some of those crimes of Borgia which to us appear the most odious would not, from causes which we have already considered, have struck an Italian of the fifteenth century with equal horror. Patriotic feeling also might induce Machiavelli to look with some indulgence and regret on the memory of the only leader who could have defended the independence of Italy against the confederate spoilers of Cambray.

On this subject Machiavelli felt most strongly. Indeed the expulsion of the foreign tyrants, and the restoration of that golden age which had preceded the irruption of Charles the Eighth, were projects which, at that time, fascinated all the master-spirits of Italy. The magnificent vision delighted the great but ill-regulated mind of Julius. It divided with manuscripts and sauces, painters, and falcons, the attention of the frivolous Leo. It prompted the generous treason of Morone. It imparted a transient energy to the feeble mind and body of the last Sforza. It excited for one moment an honest ambition in the false heart of Pescara. Ferocity and insolence were not among the vices of the national character. To the discriminating cruelties of politicians, committed for great ends on select victims, the moral code of the Italians was too indulgent. But though they might have recourse to barbarity as an expedient, they did not require it as a stimulant. They turned with loathing from the atrocity of the strangers who seemed to love blood for its own sake, who, not content with subjugating, were impatient to destroy, who found a fiendish pleasure in razing magnificent cities, cutting the throats of enemies who cried for quarter, or suffocating an unarmed population by thousands in the caverns to which it had fled for safety. Such were the cruelties which daily excited the terror and disgust of a people among whom, till lately, the worst that a soldier had to fear in a pitched battle was the loss of his horse and the expense of his ransom. The swinish intemperance of Switzerland, the wolfish avarice of Spain, the gross licentiousness of the French, indulged in violation of hospitality, of decency, of love itself, the wanton inhumanity which was common to all the invaders, had made them objects of deadly hatred to the inhabitants of the Peninsula. The wealth which had been accumulated during centuries of prosperity and repose was rapidly melting away. The intellectual superiority of the oppressed people only rendered them more keenly sensible of their political degradation. Literature and taste, indeed, still disguised with a flush of hectic loveliness and brilliancy the ravages of an incurable decay. The iron had not yet entered into the soul. The time was not yet come when eloquence was to be gagged, and reason to be hoodwinked, when the harp of the poet was to be hung on the willows of Arno, and the right hand of the painter to forget its cunning. Yet a discerning eye might even then have seen that genius and learning would not long survive the state of things from which they had sprung, and that the great men whose talents gave lustre to that melancholy period had been formed under the influence of happier days, and would leave no successors behind them. The times which shine with the greatest splendour in literary history are not always those to which the human mind is most indebted. Of this we may be convinced, by comparing the generation which follows them with that which had preceded them. The first fruits which are reaped under a bad system often spring from seed sown under a good one. Thus it was, in some measure, with the Augustan age. Thus it was with the age of Raphael and Ariosto, of Aldus and Vida.

Machiavelli deeply regretted the misfortunes of his country, and clearly discerned the cause and the remedy. It was the military system of the Italian people which had extinguished their value and discipline, and left their wealth an easy prey to every foreign plunderer. The Secretary projected a scheme alike honourable to his heart and to his intellect, for abolishing the use of mercenary troops, and for organising a national militia.

The exertions which he made to effect this great object ought alone to rescue his name from obloquy. Though his situation and his habits were pacific, he studied with intense assiduity the theory of war. He made himself master of all its details. The Florentine Government entered into his views. A council of war was appointed. Levies were decreed. The indefatigable minister flew from place to place in order to superintend the execution of his design. The times were, in some respects, favourable to the experiment. The system of military tactics had undergone a great revolution.

The cavalry was no longer considered as forming the strength of an army. The hours which a citizen could spare from his ordinary employments, though by no means sufficient to familiarise him with the exercise of a man-at-arms, might render him an useful foot-soldier. The dread of a foreign yoke, of plunder, massacre, and conflagration, might have conquered that repugnance to military pursuits which both the industry and the idleness of great towns commonly generate. For a time the scheme promised well. The new troops acquitted themselves respectably in the field. Machiavelli looked with parental rapture on the success of his plan, and began to hope that the arms of Italy might once more be formidable to the barbarians of the Tagus and the Rhine. But the tide of misfortune came on before the barriers which should have withstood it were prepared. For a time, indeed, Florence might be considered as peculiarly fortunate. Famine and sword and pestilence had devastated the fertile plains and stately cities of the Po. All the curses denounced of old against Tyre seemed to have fallen on Venice. Her merchants already stood afar off, lamenting for their great city. The time seemed near when the sea-weed should overgrow her silent Rialto, and the fisherman wash his nets in her deserted arsenal. Naples had been four times conquered and reconquered by tyrants equally indifferent to its welfare and equally greedy for its spoils. Florence, as yet, had only to endure degradation and extortion, to submit to the mandates of foreign powers, to buy over and over again, at an enormous price, what was already justly her own, to return thanks for being wronged, and to ask pardon for being in the right. She was at length deprived of the blessings even of this infamous and servile repose. Her military and political institutions were swept away together. The Medici returned, in the train of foreign invaders, from their long exile. The policy of Machiavelli was abandoned; and his public services were requited with poverty, imprisonment, and torture.

The fallen statesman still clung to his project with unabated ardour. With the view of vindicating it from some popular objections and of refuting some prevailing errors on the subject of military science, he wrote his seven books on The Art of War. This excellent work is in the form of a dialogue. The opinions of the writer are put into the mouth of Fabrizio Colonna, a powerful nobleman of the Ecclesiastical State, and an officer of distinguished merit in the service of the King of Spain. Colonna visits Florence on his way from Lombardy to his own domains. He is invited to meet some friends at the house of Cosimo Rucellai, an amiable and accomplished young man, whose early death Machiavelli feelingly deplores. After partaking of an elegant entertainment, they retire from the heat into the most shady recesses of the garden. Fabrizio is struck by the sight of some uncommon plants. Cosimo says that, though rare, in modern days, they are frequently mentioned by the classical authors, and that his grandfather, like many other Italians, amused himself with practising the ancient methods of gardening. Fabrizio expresses his regret that those who, in later times, affected the manners of the old Romans should select for imitation the most trifling pursuits. This leads to a conversation on the decline of military discipline and on the best means of restoring it. The institution of the Florentine militia is ably defended; and several improvements are suggested in the details.

The Swiss and the Spaniards were, at that time, regarded as the best soldiers in Europe. The Swiss battalion consisted of pikemen, and bore a close resemblance to the Greek phalanx. The Spaniards, like the soldiers of Rome, were armed with the sword and the shield. The victories of Flamininus and Aemilius over the Macedonian kings seem to prove the superiority of the weapons used by the legions. The same experiment had been recently tried with the same result at the battle of Ravenna, one of those tremendous days into which human folly and wickedness compress the whole devastation of a famine or a plague. In that memorable conflict, the infantry of Arragon, the old companions of Gonsalvo, deserted by all their allies, hewed a passage through the thickest of the imperial pikes, and effected an unbroken retreat, in the face of the gendarmerie of De Foix, and the renowned artillery of Este. Fabrizio, or rather Machiavelli, proposes to combine the two systems, to arm the foremost lines with the pike for the purpose of repulsing cavalry, and those in the rear with the sword, as being a weapon better adapted for every other purpose. Throughout the work, the author expresses the highest admiration of the military science of the ancient Romans, and the greatest contempt for the maxims which had been in vogue amongst the Italian commanders of the preceding generation. He prefers infantry to cavalry, and fortified camps to fortified towns. He is inclined to substitute rapid movements and decisive engagements for the languid and dilatory operations of his countrymen. He attaches very little importance to the invention of gunpowder. Indeed he seems to think that it ought scarcely to produce any change in the mode of arming or of disposing troops. The general testimony of historians, it must be allowed, seems to prove that the ill-constructed and ill-served artillery of those times, though useful in a siege, was of little value on the field of battle.

Of the tactics of Machiavelli we will not venture to give an opinion: but we are certain that his book is most able and interesting. As a commentary on the history of his times, it is invaluable. The ingenuity, the grace, and the perspicuity of the style, and the eloquence and animation of particular passages, must give pleasure even to readers who take no interest in the subject.

The Prince and the Discourses on Livy were written after the fall of the Republican Government. The former was dedicated to the young Lorenzo di Medici. This circumstance seems to have disgusted the contemporaries of the writer far more than the doctrines which have rendered the name of the work odious in later times. It was considered as an indication of political apostasy. The fact however seems to have been that Machiavelli, despairing of the liberty of Florence, was inclined to support any government which might preserve her independence. The interval which separated a democracy and a despotism, Soderini and Lorenzo, seemed to vanish when compared with the difference between the former and the present state of Italy, between the security, the opulence, and the repose which she had enjoyed under her native rulers, and the misery in which she had been plunged since the fatal year in which the first foreign tyrant had descended from the Alps. The noble and pathetic exhortation with which The Prince concludes shows how strongly the writer felt upon this subject.

The Prince traces the progress of an ambitious man, the Discourses the progress of an ambitious people. The same principles on which, in the former work, the elevation of an individual is explained, are applied in the latter, to the longer duration and more complex interest of a society. To a modern statesman the form of the Discourses may appear to be puerile. In truth Livy is not an historian on whom implicit reliance can be placed, even in cases where he must have possessed considerable means of information. And the first Decade, to which Machiavelli has confined himself, is scarcely entitled to more credit than our Chronicle of British Kings who reigned before the Roman invasion. But the commentator is indebted to Livy for little more than a few texts which he might as easily have extracted from the Vulgate or the Decameron. The whole train of thought is original.

On the peculiar immorality which has rendered The Prince unpopular, and which is almost equally discernible in the Discourses, we have already given our opinion at length. We have attempted to show that it belonged rather to the age than to the man, that it was a partial taint, and by no means implied general depravity. We cannot, however, deny that it is a great blemish, and that it considerably diminishes the pleasure which, in other respects, those works must afford to every intelligent mind.

It is, indeed, impossible to conceive a more healthful and vigorous constitution of the understanding than that which these works indicate. The qualities of the active and the contemplative statesman appear to have been blended in the mind of the writer into a rare and exquisite harmony. His skill in the details of business had not been acquired at the expense of his general powers. It had not rendered his mind less comprehensive; but it had served to correct his speculations and to impart to them that vivid and practical character which so widely distinguishes them from the vague theories of most political philosophers.

Every man who has seen the world knows that nothing is so useless as a general maxim. If it be very moral and very true, it may serve for a copy to a charity-boy. If, like those of Rochefoucault, it be sparkling and whimsical, it may make an excellent motto for an essay. But few indeed of the many wise apophthegms which have been uttered, from the time of the Seven Sages of Greece to that of Poor Richard, have prevented a single foolish action. We give the highest and the most peculiar praise to the precepts of Machiavelli when we say that they may frequently be of real use in regulating conduct, not so much because they are more just or more profound than those which might be culled from other authors, as because they can be more readily applied to the problems of real life.

There are errors in these works. But they are errors which a writer, situated like Machiavelli, could scarcely avoid. They arise, for the most part, from a single defect which appears to us to pervade his whole system. In his political scheme, the means had been more deeply considered than the ends. The great principle, that societies and laws exist only for the purpose of increasing the sum of private happiness, is not recognised with sufficient clearness. The good of the body, distinct from the good of the members, and sometimes hardly compatible with the good of the members, seems to be the object which he proposes to himself. Of all political fallacies, this has perhaps had the widest and the most mischievous operation. The state of society in the little commonwealths of Greece, the close connection and mutual dependence of the citizens, and the severity of the laws of war, tended to encourage an opinion which, under such circumstances, could hardly be called erroneous. The interests of every individual were inseparably bound up with those of the State. An invasion destroyed his corn-fields and vineyards, drove him from his home, and compelled him to encounter all the hardships of a military life. A treaty of peace restored him to security and comfort. A victory doubled the number of his slaves. A defeat perhaps made him a slave himself. When Pericles, in the Peloponnesian war, told the Athenians, that, if their country triumphed, their private losses would speedily be repaired, but, that, if their arms failed of success, every individual amongst them would probably be ruined, he spoke no more than the truth, He spoke to men whom the tribute of vanquished cities supplied with food and clothing, with the luxury of the bath and the amusements of the theatre, on whom the greatness of their Country conferred rank, and before whom the members of less prosperous communities trembled; to men who, in case of a change in the public fortunes, would, at least, be deprived of every comfort and every distinction which they enjoyed. To be butchered on the smoking ruins of their city, to be dragged in chains to a slave- market to see one child torn from them to dig in the quarries of Sicily, and another to guard the harams of Persepolis, these were the frequent and probable consequences of national calamities. Hence, among the Greeks, patriotism became a governing principle, or rather an ungovernable passion. Their legislators and their philosophers took it for granted that, in providing for the strength and greatness of the state, they sufficiently provided for the happiness of the people. The writers of the Roman empire lived under despots, into whose dominion a hundred nations were melted down, and whose gardens would have covered the little commonwealths of Phlius and Plataea. Yet they continued to employ the same language, and to cant about the duty of sacrificing everything to a country to which they owed nothing.

Causes similar to those which had influenced the disposition of the Greeks operated powerfully on the less vigorous and daring character of the Italians. The Italians, like the Greeks, were members of small communities. Every man was deeply interested in the welfare of the society to which he belonged, a partaker in its wealth and its poverty, in its glory and its shame. In the age of Machiavelli this was peculiarly the case. Public events had produced an immense sum of misery to private citizens. The Northern invaders had brought want to their boards, infamy to their beds, fire to their roofs, and the knife to their throats. It was natural that a man who lived in times like these should overrate the importance of those measures by which a nation is rendered formidable to its neighbours, and undervalue those which make it prosperous within itself.

Nothing is more remarkable in the political treatises of Machiavelli than the fairness of mind which they indicate. It appears where the author is in the wrong, almost as strongly as where he is in the right. He never advances a false opinion because it is new or splendid, because he can clothe it in a happy phrase, or defend it by an ingenious sophism. His errors are at once explained by a reference to the circumstances in which he was placed. They evidently were not sought out; they lay in his way, and could scarcely be avoided. Such mistakes must necessarily be committed by early speculators in every science.

In this respect it is amusing to compare The Prince and the Discourses with the Spirit of Laws. Montesquieu enjoys, perhaps, a wider celebrity than any political writer of modern Europe. Something he doubtless owes to his merit, but much more to his fortune. He had the good luck of a Valentine.

He caught the eye of the French nation, at the moment when it was waking from the long sleep of political and religious bigotry; and, in consequence, he became a favourite. The English, at that time, considered a Frenchman who talked about constitutional checks and fundamental laws as a prodigy not less astonishing than the learned pig or the musical infant. Specious but shallow, studious of effect, indifferent to truth, eager to build a system, but careless of collecting those materials out of which alone a sound and durable system can be built, the lively President constructed theories as rapidly and as slightly as card-houses, no sooner projected than completed, no sooner completed than blown away, no sooner blown away than forgotten. Machiavelli errs only because his experience, acquired in a very peculiar state of society, could not always enable him to calculate the effect of institutions differing from those of which he had observed the operation. Montesquieu errs, because he has a fine thing to say, and is resolved to say it. If the phaenomena which lie before him will not suit his purpose, all history must be ransacked. If nothing established by authentic testimony can be racked or chipped to suit his Procrustean hypothesis, he puts up with some monstrous fable about Siam, or Bantam, or Japan, told by writers compared with whom Lucian and

Gulliver were veracious, liars by a double right, as travellers and as Jesuits.

Propriety of thought, and propriety of diction, are commonly found together. Obscurity and affectation are the two greatest faults of style. Obscurity of expression generally springs from confusion of ideas; and the same wish to dazzle at any cost which produces affectation in the manner of a writer, is likely to produce sophistry in his reasonings. The judicious and candid mind of Machiavelli shows itself in his luminous, manly, and polished language. The style of Montesquieu, on the other hand, indicates in every page a lively and ingenious, but an unsound mind. Every trick of expression, from the mysterious conciseness of an oracle to the flippancy of a Parisian coxcomb, is employed to disguise the fallacy of some positions, and the triteness of others. Absurdities are brightened into epigrams; truisms are darkened into enigmas. It is with difficulty that the strongest eye can sustain the glare with which some parts are illuminated, or penetrate the shade in which others are concealed.

The political works of Machiavelli derive a peculiar interest from the mournful earnestness which he manifests whenever he touches on topics connected with the calamities of his native land. It is difficult to conceive any situation more painful than that of a great man, condemned to watch the lingering agony of an exhausted country, to tend it during the alternate fits of stupefaction and raving which precede its dissolution, and to see the symptoms of vitality disappear one by one, till nothing is left but coldness, darkness, and corruption. To this joyless and thankless duty was Machiavelli called. In the energetic language of the prophet, he was "mad for the sight of his eye which he saw," disunion in the council, effeminacy in the camp, liberty extinguished, commerce decaying, national honour sullied, an enlightened and flourishing people given over to the ferocity of ignorant savages. Though his opinions had no escaped the contagion of that political immorality which was common among his countrymen, his natural disposition seem to have been rather stern and impetuous than pliant and artful When the misery and degradation of Florence and the foul outrage which he had himself sustained recur to his mind, the smooth craft of his profession and his nation is exchanged for the honest bitterness of scorn and anger. He speaks like one sick of the calamitous times and abject people among whom his lot is cast. He pines for the strength and glory of ancient Rome, for the fasces of Brutus, and the sword of Scipio, the gravity of the curule chair, and the bloody pomp of the triumphal sacrifice. He seems to be transported back to the days when eight hundred thousand Italian warriors sprung to arms at the rumour of a Gallic invasion. He breathes all the spirit of those intrepid and haughty senators who forgot the dearest ties of nature in the claims of public duty, who looked with disdain on the elephants and on the gold of Pyrrhus, and listened with unaltered composure to the tremendous tidings of Cannae. Like an ancient temple deformed by the barbarous architecture of a later age, his character acquires an interest from the very circumstances which debase it. The original proportions are rendered more striking by the contrast which they present to the mean and incongruous additions.

The influence of the sentiments which we have described was not apparent in his writings alone. His enthusiasm, barred from the career which it would have selected for itself, seems to have found a vent in desperate levity. He enjoyed a vindictive pleasure in outraging the opinions of a society which he despised. He became careless of the decencies which were expected from a man so highly distinguished in the literary and political world. The sarcastic bitterness of his conversation disgusted those who were more inclined to accuse his licentiousness than their own degeneracy, and who were unable to conceive the strength of those emotions which are concealed by the jests of the wretched, and by the follies of the wise.

The historical works of Machiavelli still remain to be considered. The Life of Castruccio Castracani will occupy us for a very short time, and would scarcely have demanded our notice, had it not attracted a much greater share of public attention than it deserves. Few books, indeed, could be more interesting than a careful and judicious account, from such a pen, of the illustrious Prince of Lucca, the most eminent of those Italian chiefs who, like Pisistratus and Gelon, acquired a power felt rather than seen, and resting, not on law or on prescription, but on the public favour and on their great personal qualities. Such a work would exhibit to us the real nature of that species of sovereignty, so singular and so often misunderstood, which the Greeks denominated tyranny, and which, modified in some degree by the feudal system, reappeared in the commonwealths of Lombardy and Tuscany. But this little composition of Machiavelli is in no sense a history. It has no pretensions to fidelity. It is a trifle, and not a very successful trifle. It is scarcely more authentic than the novel of Belphegor, and is very much duller.

The last great work of this illustrious man was the history of his native city. It was written by command of the Pope, who, as chief of the house of Medici, was at that time sovereign of Florence. The

116

characters of Cosmo, of Piero, and of Lorenzo, are, however, treated with a freedom and impartiality equally honourable to the writer and to the patron. The miseries and humiliations of dependence, the bread which is more bitter than every other food, the stairs which are more painful than every other ascent, had not broken the spirit of Machiavelli. The most corrupting post in a corrupting profession had not depraved the generous heart of Clement.

The History does not appear to be the fruit of much industry or research. It is unquestionably inaccurate. But it is elegant, lively, and picturesque, beyond any other in the Italian language. The reader, we believe, carries away from it a more vivid and a more faithful impression of the national character and manners than from more correct accounts. The truth is, that the book belongs rather to ancient than to modern literature. It is in the style, not of Davila and Clarendon, but of Herodotus and Tacitus. The classical histories may almost be called romances founded in fact. The relation is, no doubt, in all its principal points, strictly true. But the numerous little incidents which heighten the interest, the words, the gestures, the looks, are evidently furnished by the imagination of the author. The fashion of later times is different. A more exact narrative is given by the writer. It may be doubted whether more exact notions are conveyed to the reader. The best portraits are perhaps those in which there is a slight mixture of caricature, and we are not certain that the best histories are not those in which a little of the exaggeration of fictitious narrative is judiciously employed. Something is lost in accuracy; but much is gained in effect. The fainter lines are neglected but the great characteristic features are imprinted on the mind for ever.

The History terminates with the death of Lorenzo de' Medici. Machiavelli had, it seems, intended to continue his narrative to a later period. But his death prevented the execution of his design; and the melancholy task of recording the desolation and shame of Italy devolved on Guicciardini.

Machiavelli lived long enough to see the commencement of the last struggle for Florentine liberty. Soon after his death monarchy was finally established, not such a monarchy as that of which Cosmo had laid the foundations deep in the institution and feelings of his countryman, and which Lorenzo had embellished with the trophies of every science and every art; but a loathsome tyranny, proud and mean, cruel and feeble, bigoted and lascivious. The character of Machiavelli was hateful to the new masters of Italy; and those parts of his theory which were in strict accordance with their own daily practice afforded a pretext for blackening his memory. His works were misrepresented by the learned, misconstrued by the ignorant, censured by the Church, abused with all the rancour of simulated virtue by the tools of a base government, and the priests of a baser superstition. The name of the man whose genius had illuminated all the dark places of policy, and to whose patriotic wisdom an oppressed people had owed their last chance of emancipation and revenge, passed into a proverb of infamy. For more than two hundred years his bones lay undistinguished. At length, an English nobleman paid the as honours to the greatest statesman of Florence. In the church of Santa Croce a monument was erected to his memory, which is contemplated with reverence by all who can distinguish the virtues of a great mind through the corruptions of a degenerate age, and which will be approached with still deeper homage when the object to which his public life was devoted shall be attained, when the foreign yoke shall be broken, when a second Procida shall avenge the wrongs of Naples, when a happier Rienzi shall restore the good estate of Rome, when the streets of Florence and Bologna shall again resound with their ancient war-cry, Popolo; popolo; muoiano i tiranni!